DINE OLDENBURG SEGAL

painting / sculpture

ART GALLERY OF ONTARIO — January 14 - February 12, 1967

ALBRIGHT-KNOX ART GALLERY — February 24 - March 26, 1967

LIST OF LENDERS

Harry N. Abrams Family Collection, *New York*
Mr and Mrs Roger Davidson, *Toronto*
Mr and Mrs Jim Dine, Ithaca, *New York*
Jeremy, Matthew, and Nicholas Dine, *Ithaca*, New York
Mr and Mrs Marvin Goodman, *Toronto*
Mr and Mrs S. Allen Guiberson, *Dallas*
Ellen Johnson, *Oberlin, Ohio*
Mr and Mrs D. Franklin Königsberg, *New York*
Mrs Phyllis Lambert, *New York*
Mr and Mrs Claes Oldenburg, *New York*
Mary Sisler Collection, *New York*
Alan Solomon, *New York*
Mr and Mrs Richard Solomon, *Boston*
Mr and Mrs Burton Tremaine, *Meriden, Connecticut*
Dr and Mrs Sydney L. Wax, *Toronto*

Albright-Knox Art Gallery, *Buffalo*
Allen Memorial Art Museum, Oberlin College, *Oberlin, Ohio*
Art Gallery of Ontario, *Toronto*
Whitney Museum of American Art, *New York*

Sidney Janis Gallery, *New York*

ACKNOWLEDGEMENTS

Our first thanks must go to the lenders whose generosity has allowed us to present a selection of works of high quality. Mr Sidney Janis has contributed greatly to the exhibition by making available many works from his Gallery. The artists have been especially cooperative throughout the preparation for this exhibition, and we particularly appreciate their designing the half-title pages for the catalogue.

We owe much to Ellen H. Johnson, Alan Solomon and Robert Pincus-Witten for kindly consenting to write informative and illuminating articles on the three artists and for their advice on the selection of the works.

We are also indebted to Richard Bellamy, who provided information about the early works, Nathan Rabin, who did much of the photography, and Alan Suddon, who helped with the bibliography.

The Art Gallery of Ontario is pleased to share the *Dine / Oldenburg / Segal* exhibition with the Albright-Knox Art Gallery. We are grateful to the Director, Mr Gordon Smith, and the Assistant Director, Mr Samuel Miller, for their enthusiastic support and cooperation.

The Curator of Modern Art of the Art Gallery of Ontario, Brydon Smith, organized the exhibition and edited this catalogue. He was assisted by members of the staff particularly David Brooke, Charles McFaddin, Eva Robinson and Margaret Ashton. Very special thanks must be extended to Frank Newfeld who designed the catalogue.

Finally we are very grateful to The Canada Council for the financial assistance which made both the exhibition and catalogue possible.

WILLIAM J. WITHROW
Director
Art Gallery of Ontario

Jim Dine, Claes Oldenburg and George Segal are three very individual artists, but they share some characteristics in their art. All three use ordinary objects familiar to everyone, but each artist assimilates them so completely into his work that the objects momentarily lose their ordinariness. Within their new framework, the objects become visually and psychologically expressive of the artist's feelings or fantasies. Dine, Oldenburg and Segal are, in varying degrees, (as Alan Solomon states in his article on Jim Dine) 'hot' artists.

Their choice of banal and popular images would seem to link them with pop artists Roy Lichtenstein and Andy Warhol, but these two artists duplicate their chosen images in a mechanical manner of painting, to simulate the mass-produced technique of their original source. Warhol summed up his feelings about his use of silk-screen printing in his statement, "The reason I'm painting this way is that I want to be a machine", and Lichtenstein has said, "The impersonal look is what I wanted to have." This mechanical and impersonal approach makes the viewer unable to be sure of Warhol's and Lichtenstein's feelings about the subjects of their paintings. They appear to be uncommitted or 'cool' artists.

Dine, Oldenburg and Segal share, as well as an underlying expressionism, a similar development in their art from painting into sculpture. All three started as painters and in the late 1950's began to extend the flat visual space of the painting to fill or take in parts of the surrounding space. This bold use of the space in front of the canvas led Dine and Oldenburg to initiate a number of happenings in the late 1950's and early 1960's. Happenings involving movement, costumes, sounds, lights, objects, scents and colours surrounded not only the artists and other performers but also the spectators.

Dine has said that his happenings were extensions of his life and his painting and through happenings he could reach people more directly than he could through painting alone. Dine stopped doing happenings in 1960 when they were becoming fashionable (with the exception of *Natural History [Dreams],* N.Y.C., April 1965), since he felt that the temporary presentation of an art form which was for him so closely allied with his life only confused the spectator about the artist's intentions.

When he returned to painting fulltime, he incorporated into his paintings real objects with very personal associations. Attached to his paintings, these large objects project boldly out towards the viewer. Sometimes he paints the objects so that their surface forms relate visually to the canvas; more often, the objects are not painted but are dramatically contrasted to the painted surface of the canvas. These objects create an intense interaction with the viewer, who finds it physically and psychologically difficult to see the objects purely as forms or as art. While using objects to provoke the direct confrontation that he discovered in his happenings, at the same time Dine has continued to paint traditionally, using oil on canvas. He uses objects formally as catalysts for his painting.

When Dine turned to cast aluminum sculpture in 1965/66, he continued to explore the emotive effect of single isolated objects, either cast from things such as the *Double Right Handed Doorway* (no. 15), which is a cast of his own right arm (because he is left-handed), or things created in his mind and given form outside it such as *Another Ribbon Machine* (no. 16).

Oldenburg's happenings of the early 1960's were, like Dine's happenings, extensions of his paintings and sculptures, and were part of his general concern at the time to use more or less altered "real" objects. At first, Oldenburg dreamed up the subjects of his sculpture: *Empire Papa Ray Gun* (no. 26) and *Street Head* (no. 27) shaped out of *papier mâché,* burlap and refuse. Later he chose less personal subjects (hamburgers, sodas, electric outlets and appliances), but they were still shaped out of plaster, wood, cardboard and soft materials. To all of his materials, except vinyl, he adds texture and a personal touch by painting the surface. Even his soft vinyl pieces retain in the folds the fluid painterliness of his more traditional painted works. One reason Oldenburg gives for his break with painting is that he wants to give a concrete statement to his fantasy and "instead of painting it, to make it touchable, to translate the eye into the fingers."

It is unfortunate that Segal's early sculptures and paintings were not available for this exhibition, for the extension of painting into sculpture is most literal and decisive in his work. Describing his three figures of 1958 made out of wire, plaster and burlap, Segal said "they looked to me as if they had stepped out of my paintings." Some of his canvases at the time contained life-size figures drawn in charcoal on raw canvas. The dry cloth texture of these figures is very similar to the plaster-soaked cloth surfaces of his sculpture. In turn, the drips and splatters of plaster on the surface of the sculpture figures is a retention of his expressionist paint handling, and in his works done after 1961, such as *Man Sitting at Table* (no. 48), this fluid painterly surface contrasts with the real objects.

Although Segal did not present any happenings himself, he was a close friend of the originator of happenings, Allan Kaprow, who performed one of his first happenings on Segal's chicken farm. His figures, because they are life-size and significantly posed in an everyday activity, evoke a sense of drama, which is heightened by the theatrical settings. Segal's inclusion of only a few objects important to the figure's activity forces the viewer to concentrate on the whole scene or action rather than individual inert objects.

In much of their painting and sculpture since 1960, Dine, Oldenburg and Segal have used objects or easily recognizable altered objects, thereby setting up for the viewer a startling interplay between the real and the unreal, between the ordinary and the extraordinary.

The interplay between the real and the unreal becomes in Segal's pieces a life-giving interaction. His sculpture is not a record of what a sculptor sees, but rather a real postural duplicate of the model. Confronted with a Segal sculpture, the viewer's sense of sight rejects the plaster figure as unreal, but because the objects of the figure's environment have been used and lived with, the figure gathers into itself the sense of life which still resides in the objects. The plaster figure, which is a physical exoskeleton of a person, functions in an ordinary way like the stand-in worshippers of 3000 B.C. Sumeria. These stone sculptures were carved to represent an individual and to worship in the temple on his behalf. In an age which has rationalized the magic out of religion, Segal's stand-ins dutifully fulfil their destinies in secular environments.

Dine's work, especially since 1961, has emphasized a constant physical and psychological interplay between the real objects and the paint surface. In *Black Bathroom #2* (no. 9) there is a visual pun between the painted shadow to the right of the chrome drain pipe and the real shadows which the drain pipe casts onto the canvas surface. This subtle shadow play between art and reality is carried to its conclusion in the disturbing but sensitive *The Chrome Lite, The Silverpoint Jacket* (no. 13). Because this silverpoint drawing has its own light source, the shadow cast by the metal hook coincides with its drawn counterpart, blending the real and unreal. Dine has called the canvas "the last vestige of unreality", for it allows him to take over and re-present utilitarian objects in the context of useless art.

Oldenburg finds in common objects equivalents of his fantasies. Through his careful metamorphosis of objects he is able to shape his fantasies into concrete and tangible forms, which can have an hallucinatory effect on the viewer.

Because his objects represent his fantasies, and because his objects, such as the tubs (nos. 36, 37 and 38) and engine parts (no. 35), have a nonfunctional resemblance to the original image, Oldenburg has called himself a technological liar. Reminded of Cézanne's praise of Monet ("Monet is only an eye, but, heavens, what an eye!"), one can only add, what a liar!

The half-title pages which the three artists designed for this catalogue sum up graphically their individual approaches to their subject matter. Dine has selected, for its silhouette, a reproduction of an object from his recent *A Tool Box* series of prints and has attached it emphatically to the page. Oldenburg, more traditionally using crayon and wash, has created new forms based on drainpipes or the idea of drainpipes. Segal, by xeroxing his driver's licence, has duplicated in ghost fashion a part of his own body-image.

The introductory articles for each artist in this catalogue are as individual in their approach as the artists themselves. Alan Solomon has written a personal article on Dine which illuminates his attitude to his work, as well as the viewer's response to it; Ellen Johnson describes Oldenburg's development with sensitive and clear interpretations of works in the exhibition; Robert Pincus-Witten illustrates Segal's development by tracing the history of critical reaction to his paintings and sculptures.

BRYDON SMITH
Curator of Modern Art

Jim Dine

Jim Dine

Born in Cincinnati, Ohio, June 16, 1935.
Studied at the University of Cincinnati and the Boston Museum School.
B.F.A. Ohio University, 1957.
Graduate work at Ohio University, 1958.
Moved to New York, 1959.
Guest lecturer at Yale University, spring 1965.
Artist-in-residence at Oberlin College, November 1965.
Visited London, England, for 6 weeks, spring 1966.
Presently is Visiting Critic in the College of Architecture, Cornell University, Ithaca, New York.

Jim Dine:

hot artist in a cool time

After his work, Jim Dine turns out to be something of a surprise, until the relationship between the person and the art begins to become clear. Animated and responsive, turned on almost to the point of hyperesthesia, he is the kind of man people respond to intensely, so that either they like him very much, or else he makes them terribly nervous, depending on how they react to his psychic stresses, which he carries about with him in a more overt way than most of us are inclined to. Self-conscious about his person, with that extraordinary bald head and the shortish figure tending to obesity, he is something of a dandy, and really believes that he would like to be an actor. He demonstrates certain natural skills in this direction socially, and in his happenings, where he had an unbelievably charismatic effect. (I suppose he has fantasies about acting being much easier than painting, just as all the actors we know would like to be something else easier, like an artist; but more than this it has something to do with his strong impulse toward more direct contact with his audience, which shows up in his work in a variety of ways.)

His fastidiousness and his social facility seem very much at odds with his art; he comes on much more like an aspirant to the bourgeoisie than the author of those often strange and gritty works which appear to flaunt all the traditional values of art, which are often so messy and nasty, which precariously skirt the edge of everything (psychologically) menacing, disruptive, and irritating, and which may seem to be the products of a disassociated and antagonistic personality.

But then one realizes that it is all worked out in the paintings, that as much as he aims to displease (in conventional terms) in his art, he is that winning as a person, and the art is really about wanting to shake us up and make us share his intense involvement and his commitment and his excitement in the marginal realm of feeling where the deepest echoes resound to all that half-felt half-known heightened reality where joy reigns and frustration and repression give way.

He aims for modes to express those depths, where art can be a release from the tensions and the agonies which complicate all our lives on the familiar mundane levels; he hovers between apprehension and sublimation, between anxiety and euphoria, living his art and turning the hundred intimate details of his life and feeling into paintings and drawings and prints and sculpture.

He reminds me of Picasso. Not in any superficial terms of style, nor do I mean to imply any correspondence in the meaning of their lives or work.

Like Picasso, he is obsessive; he works, he draws obsessively: this means the activity is a significant source of gratification for him. Like Picasso, he draws sequentially, working with undiminished invention through marvelously subtle and ever-fresh variations on single images, doing long series on the same theme, which give him untold pleasure, just in the sheer doing, and in the complication and variation of ideas. Such men belong to a chosen group. They have outlets almost beyond the comprehension of the rest of us, who struggle for a few brief moments of gratification and fulfillment. It is really quite difficult to think of many people in one's experience to whom this kind of appeasement of desire in habitual activity is available, for whom work brings such special joy. More than the result of a happy accident, the opportunity seems to be tied to a certain quality of accessibility to experience and feeling.

Alan Solomon

Since work gives him so much satisfaction ("Drawing is like eating a good meal"), Dine turns most readily to ideas and formal analogies with familiar objects which are essentially sexual in meaning ("This is the area to which my thoughts most naturally turn, and the kind of subject with which I feel most comfortable and familiar"). It is not a matter of exposing us to his own erotic sentiments; rather it hinges on a desire to express the richness and ambiguity of the role objects play in our feelings, at the deepest and most meaningful level, and particularly at the level of our sexual sensibility. This brings up certain problems which at the moment have a special relevance.

Among the radical changes which have taken place in our world in the past few years one of the least dramatic but most important has been the change in our attitude toward the details of human feeling and behaviour. Through most of the past since classical times, we have applied a double standard to the expression of many thoughts and feelings and the discussion of many acts which are nevertheless common to all of us, particularly in matters that have to do with sex. It has been customary, for instance, to pretend that sexual feelings do not occupy a significant part of the consciousness of most people, and to pretend that we do not have the habit of finding sexual analogies in all kinds of familiar situations, or that many of our patterns of thinking are not determined by unconscious reference to these sexual analogies. A recent example of what I mean that comes to mind at the moment is the scheme worked out by American space engineers for the docking of the Gemini capsule with the Agena rocket. It seems certain enough that a significantly different arrangement might well have been devised by female engineers, and that the fascination which we all shared in following this particular detail of the adventure had something to do with our conscious or unconscious acknowledgement of the sexual analogy.

Until very recently, it has been our custom to suppress such feelings, experiencing them but pretending that they did not exist, for reasons which are irrational but familiar, going back as they do to the roots of the Judeo-Christian tradition. Now it has become increasingly possible to deal more openly with these feelings, and to acknowledge that some of our artists who are accustomed to expressing themselves more freely without repression have been habitually dealing with sexuality without descending to obscenity or pornography.

Of course this progress is only partial; even as I write, a group of collage drawings by Dine has been confiscated by the police from an exhibition in London on grounds of obscenity, apparently because they contain flesh coloured forms which may be read as distinctly genital in character (or not). The problem is that no matter how sophisticated we may pretend to be about these questions, the explicitness of graphic representation threatens to stir our senses more than any other mode of expression. There is a long tradition of avoidance of such subjects among major artists in their public work, although we know that many of them privately produced erotic art. (I do not discuss the extensive history of the paintings of nudes, which we treat as if they were not always motivated by erotic considerations.) More recently, although literature has been gradually emancipated, and book banning virtually suspended, we have felt compelled to proceed very deliberately and cautiously in the areas of film and the visual arts.

Another event of this moment has been the exhibition of erotic art at the Sidney Janis Gallery in New York, where the prurient were largely disappointed, because it turns out that serious artists always approach their subject matter in complex and ambiguous ways, whether it is about sex or not. In the absence of scatological intention, and in the presence of a kind of innocent, intense openness, sexual subjects in the end turn out to stand or fall on their own merits, like everything else.

Despite these complications and setbacks, the plain fact is that at this point we can at least acknowledge the presence of such considerations in art. The very fact that the problem requires so much discussion in a sense distorts its meaning and its importance, and I do not intend to imply that the expression of sexual feeling is the sole issue in Dine's art. The attention he pays to this kind of subject comes out of his awareness of it as a critical realm of tenuous interaction between the pressure of feelings and the demands of functioning in our given cultural context. In other words, sex is an area peculiarly suited to the climate of psychic tension Dine means to create in his art. It must be understood in one sense that if his paintings did not generate this combination of anxiety and excitement they would not give him so much pleasure to produce. Making art thus becomes for Dine, as in the case of Picasso, a constantly renewing cathartic process which the artist invites us to share.

All this is part of a new heightened sense of the role our younger artists want to assign to their work. Art has become a deadly serious business, at the same time that it has become consciously playful (like so much of Dine's work), humorous, and an acknowledged source of gratification. It is intended to impinge on our lives much more extensively than in the past, as part of our growing awareness of the possibilities of augmented modes of consciousness, beyond the conventionally assumed limits of reality.

One might say that Dine has pressed this issue more ruthlessly than some of his contemporaries, less sparingly with respect to our old-fashioned sensibilities and emotional habits. It seems desperately important to him for us to mend our ways, to enlarge our viewpoints, to become more accessible to the variety of experience which the radical contemporary alterations in esthetic values have exposed to us.

While he shares these goals with a number of his contemporaries, he differs from many of them in his sense of the necessity to lay one's emotional cards on the table. In this respect, he is a 'hot' artist, like Oldenburg and Segal. Perhaps this has something to do with their original ties to expressionism (they matured earlier than their cool contemporaries). The stylistic evidence of these origins has largely disappeared from Dine's art, but the full force of his bias toward passion continues to assert itself, at a time when many other artists with different temperaments have assumed a more neutral and passive aspect.

CATALOGUE OF WORKS BY JIM DINE

1 *Green Suit.* 1959.
Oil and cloth, 65⅝ x 28¾ in.
Collection the artist.

2 *Shoes Walking on My Brain.* 1960.
Oil, cloth and shoes, 40 x 36 x 6 in.
Mr Alan Solomon.

3 *Three Growing Rainbows.* 1960.
Oil on canvas and rope, 60 x 108 in.
(3 panels, each 60 x 36 in.).
Mr and Mrs D. Franklin Königsberg.

4 *Tie Tie.* 1961.
Oil on canvas, 70 x 70 in.
Mary Sisler collection.

5 *Shovel.* 1962.
Oil on canvas, shovel, box and dirt,
96 x 38 in.
Mr Alan Solomon.

6 *Crescent Wrench.* 1962.
Oil on canvas and wood, nuts,
bolts and wrench, 60 x 50 in.
Mr and Mrs Burton Tremaine.

7 *Four Rooms.* 1962.
Oil on canvas, metal, rubber and
upholstered chair, 72 x 180 in.
Sidney Janis Gallery.

8 *Child's Blue Wall.* 1962.
Oil on canvas, wood, metal and
light bulb, 60 x 72 in.
Albright-Knox Art Gallery, Buffalo,
gift of Seymour H. Knox.

9 *Black Bathroom #2.* 1962.
Oil and drawing on canvas and
china washbasin, 72 x 72 in.
Art Gallery of Ontario, Toronto,
gift of Mr and Mrs M. H. Rapp, 1966.

10 *In My Cincinnati Studio.* 1963.
Oil on canvas, 72 x 96 in.
Mr and Mrs S. Allen Guiberson.

11 *2 Palettes in Black with Stovepipe.* 1963.
Oil on canvas and stovepipe,
left panel: 84½ x 72 in.,
right panel: 51 x 33½ in.
Sidney Janis Gallery.

12 *Double Red Self Portrait*
(The Green Lines.) 1964.
Oil on canvas and mixed media,
84 x 120 in.
Mrs Phyllis B. Lambert.

13 *The Chrome Lite,*
The Silverpoint Jacket. 1964.
Silverpoint on canvas with metal lamp,
72 x 51 in.
Collection the artist.

14 *The Long Boot.* 1965.
Cast aluminum, 118¼ x 12 x 4 in.
Harry N. Abrams Family Collection.

15 *Double Right Handed Doorway.* 1965.
Cast aluminum, 88½ x 35½ x 10 in.
Sidney Janis Gallery.

16 *Another Ribbon Machine.* 1965.
Cast aluminum and coloured ribbons,
73½ x 69 x 10 in.
Sidney Janis Gallery.

17 *Angels for Lorca.* 1966.
Fiberglas and cast aluminum,
3 pieces, each 73 x 24 in.
Sidney Janis Gallery.

DRAWINGS

18 *Smash, Bash, Gash, Crash,*
Crash, Smash, Crack. 1960.
White ink on black paper, 23 x 37 in.
Mr Alan Solomon.

19 *One Orange Toothbrush.* 1962.
Collage, 20 x 30 in.
Harry N. Abrams Family Collection.

20 *4 Chairs #12.* 1962.
Collage, 18 x 24 in.
Sidney Janis Gallery.

21 *Hammer Bunches.* 1962-63.
India ink, crayon and fixative on paper,
55⅝ x 42$\frac{3}{16}$ in.
Jeremy, Matthew and Nicholas Dine.

22 *Palette (Joan) #2.* 1964.
Pencil, cloth and candy on paper,
24 x 18 in.
Nancy Dine.

23 *3 Pearl Studs.* 1965.
Collage and cloth, 33 x 18 in.
Sidney Janis Gallery.

24 *Untitled.* 1965.
Charcoal on paper, 40⅜ x 27¼ in.
Allen Memorial Art Museum,
Oberlin College, Oberlin.

Green Suit
1959 Oil and cloth,
65⅝ x 28¾ in.
Collection the artist

If you can
make it in life —
and I don't say
that's easy to do —
then you can
make it with art.

Shoes Walking on My Brain
1960 Oil, cloth and shoes, 40 x 36 x 6 in.
Mr Alan Solomon

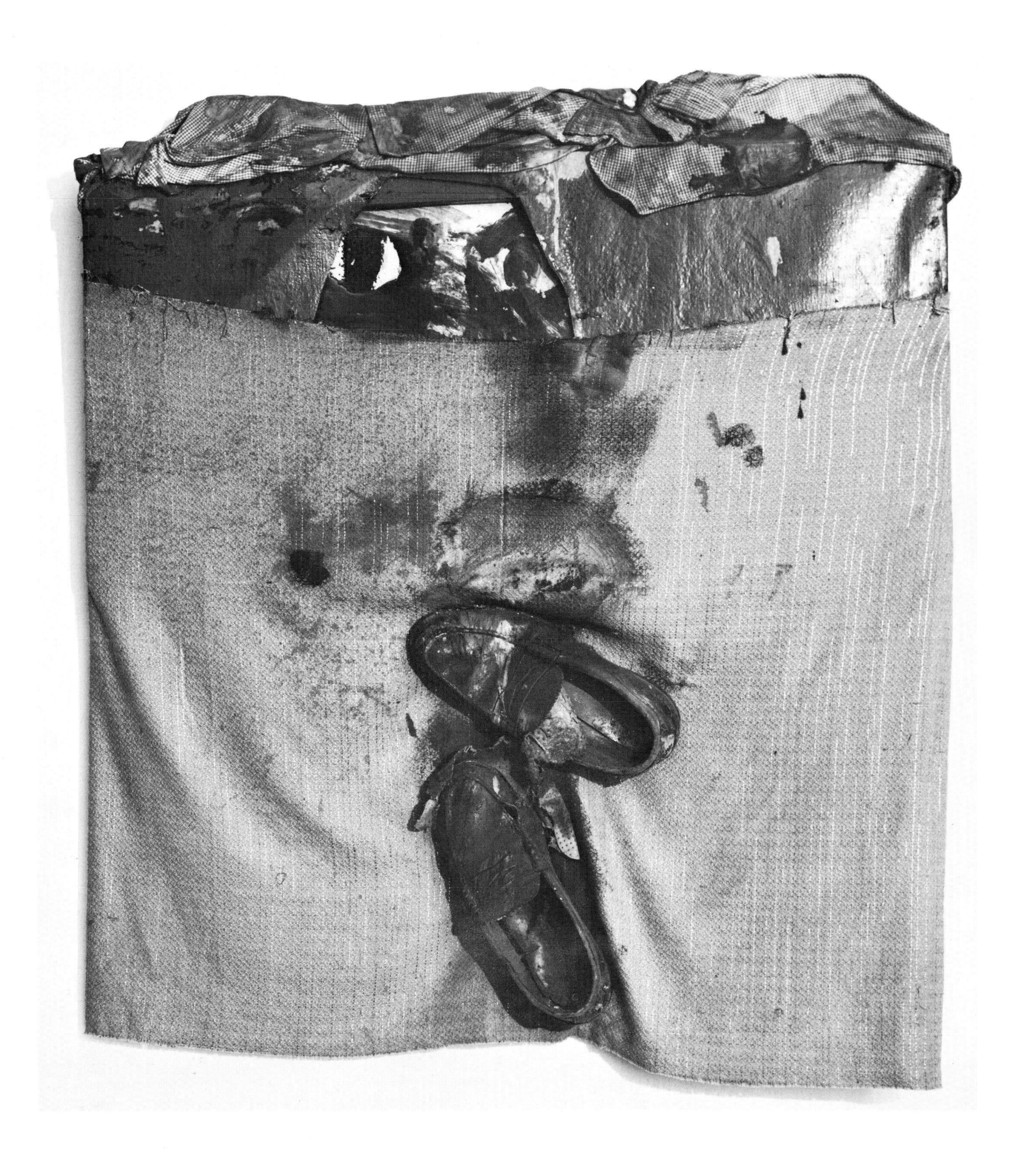

Three Growing Rainbows
1960 Oil on canvas and rope, 60 x 108 in.
(3 panels, each 60 x 36 in.)
Mr and Mrs D. Franklin Königsberg

Tie Tie 1961 Oil on canvas, 70 x 70 in. Mary Sisler collection

Shovel
1962
Oil on canvas,
shovel, box and dirt,
96 x 38 in.
Mr Alan Solomon

Crescent Wrench
1962 Oil on canvas and wood, nuts, bolts and wrench, 60 x 50 in.
Mr and Mrs Burton Tremaine

Four Rooms 1962 Oil on canvas, metal, rubber and upholstered chair, 72 x 180 in. Sidney Janis Gallery

Child's Blue Wall
1962
Oil on canvas, wood, metal and light bulb, 60 x 72 in.
Albright-Knox Art Gallery, Buffalo,
gift of Seymour H. Knox

Black Bathroom #2

1962 Oil and drawing on canvas and china washbasin, 72 x 72 in.
Art Gallery of Ontario, Toronto,
gift of Mr and Mrs M. H. Rapp, 1966

The painting that has the sink in it, Black Bathroom #2 . . .
*that really is just a drawing. That thing works as a negative space,
but nobody gets past that sink. Nobody wants to get past it.
They want to harp on the sink, they want to wash their hands in the sink,
they want water to come out of it. Art does not work that way.
Art is not a game.*

In My Cincinnati Studio
1963
Oil on canvas, 72 x 96 in.
Mr and Mrs S. Allen Guiberson

If it's art, who cares if it's a comment?

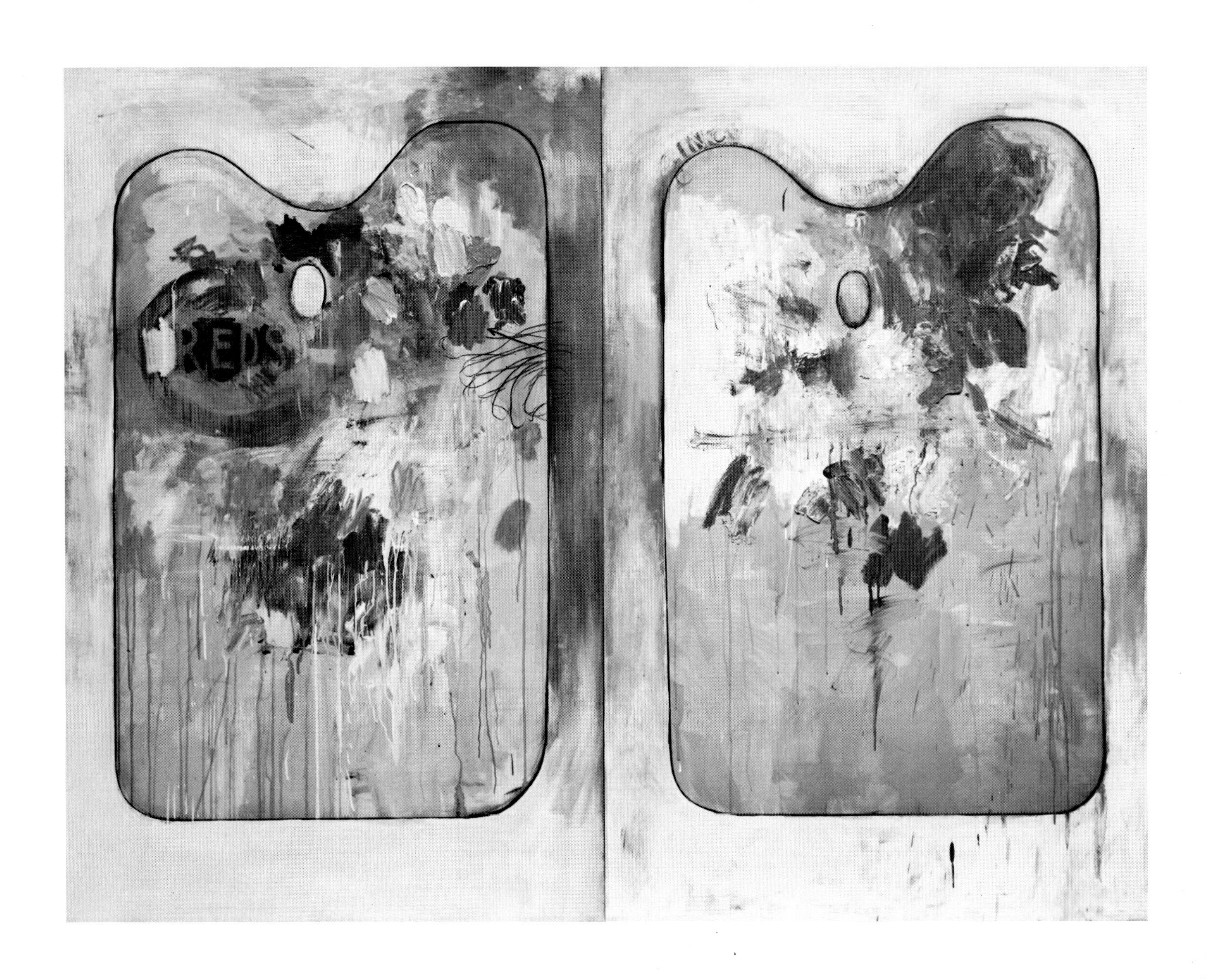

2 Palettes in Black with Stovepipe
1963 Oil on canvas and stovepipe,
left panel: 84½ x 72 in., right panel: 51 x 33½ in.
Sidney Janis Gallery

I'm working on a series of palettes right now.
I put down the palette first; then people can walk over it,
I can put a hammer in the middle of it . . .
Every time I do something, the whole thing becomes richer;
it is another thing added to the landscape.

Double Red Self Portrait (The Green Lines)
1964
Oil on canvas and mixed media, 84 x 120 in.
Mrs Phyllis B. Lambert

The Chrome Lite, The Silverpoint Jacket
1964
Silverpoint on canvas with metal lamp, 72 x 51 in.
Collection the artist

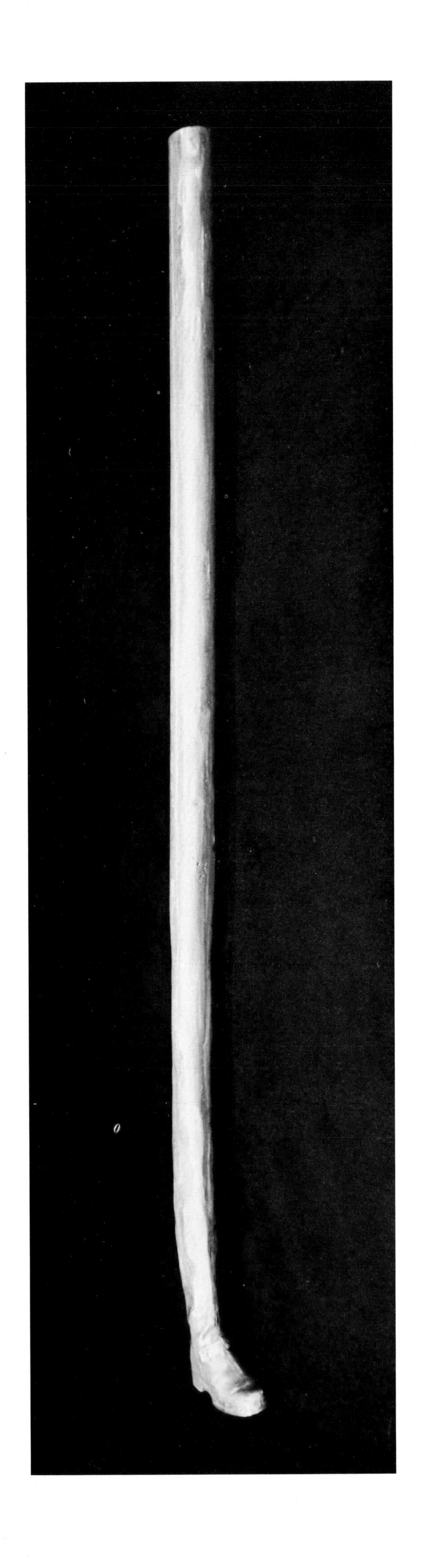

The Long Boot
1965
Cast aluminum,
118¼ x 12 x 4 in.
Harry N. Abrams
Family Collection

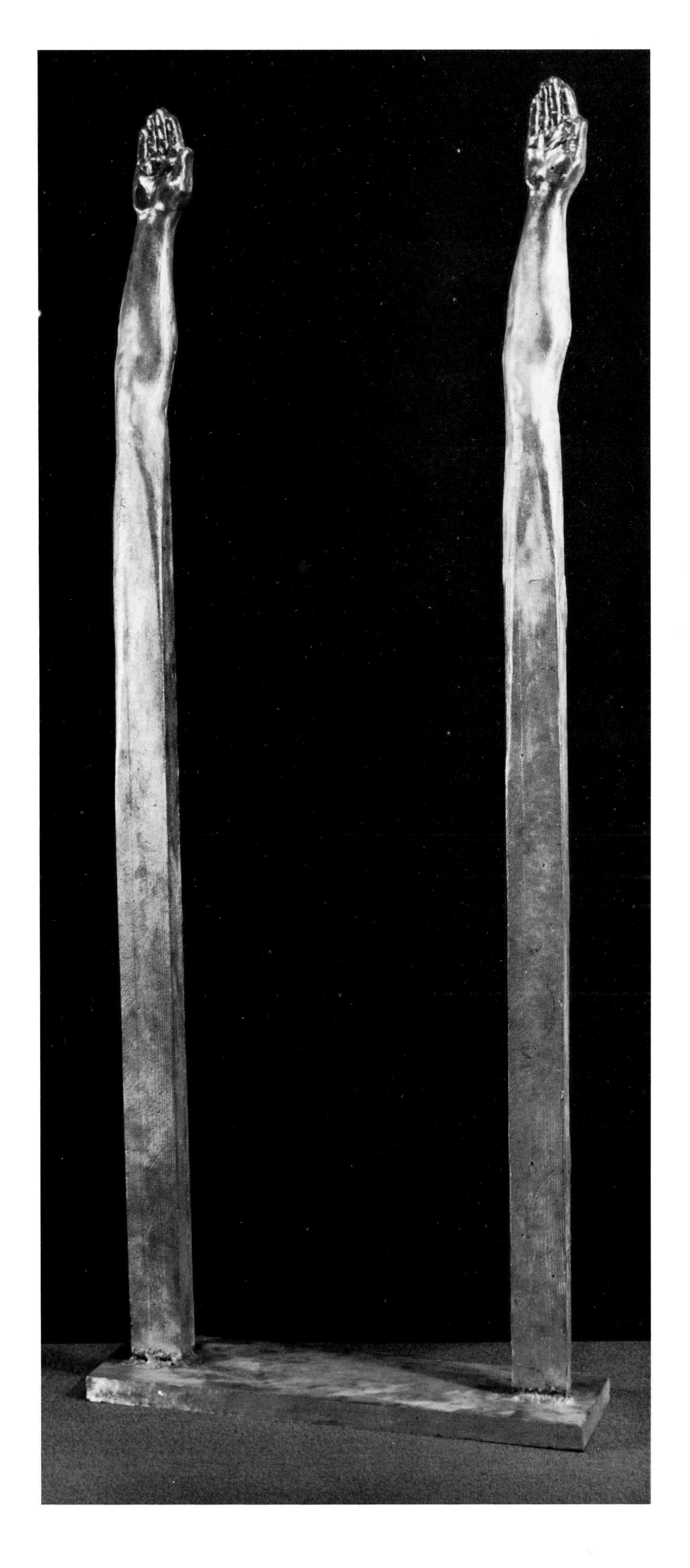

Double Right Handed Doorway
1965
Cast aluminum,
88½ x 35½ x 10 in.
Sidney Janis Gallery

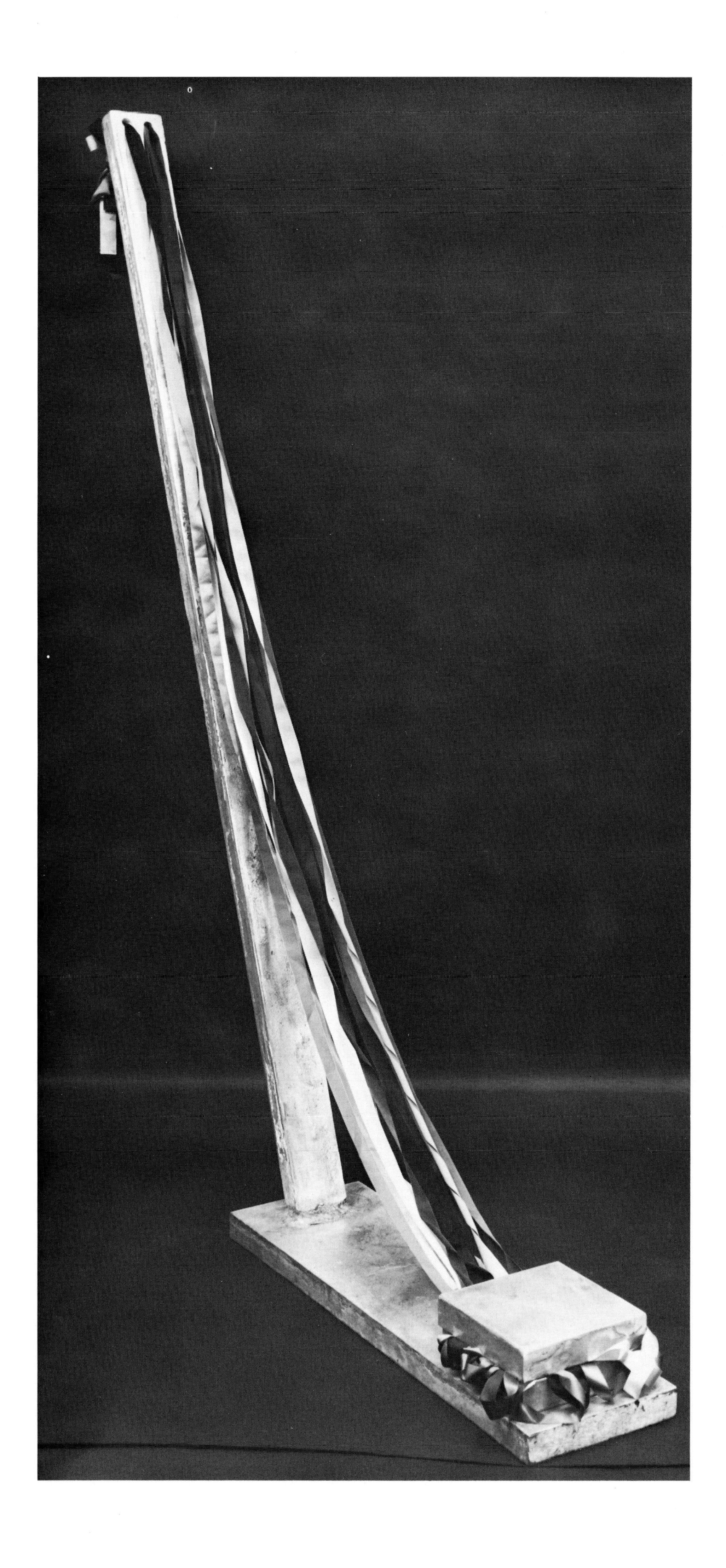

Another Ribbon Machine
1965
Cast aluminum and coloured ribbons,
73½ x 69 x 10 in.
Sidney Janis Gallery

Angels for Lorca
1966
Fiberglas and cast aluminum,
3 pieces,
each 73 x 24 in.
Sidney Janis Gallery
OPPOSITE

3 Pearl Studs
1965
Collage and cloth, 33 x 18 in.
Sidney Janis Gallery

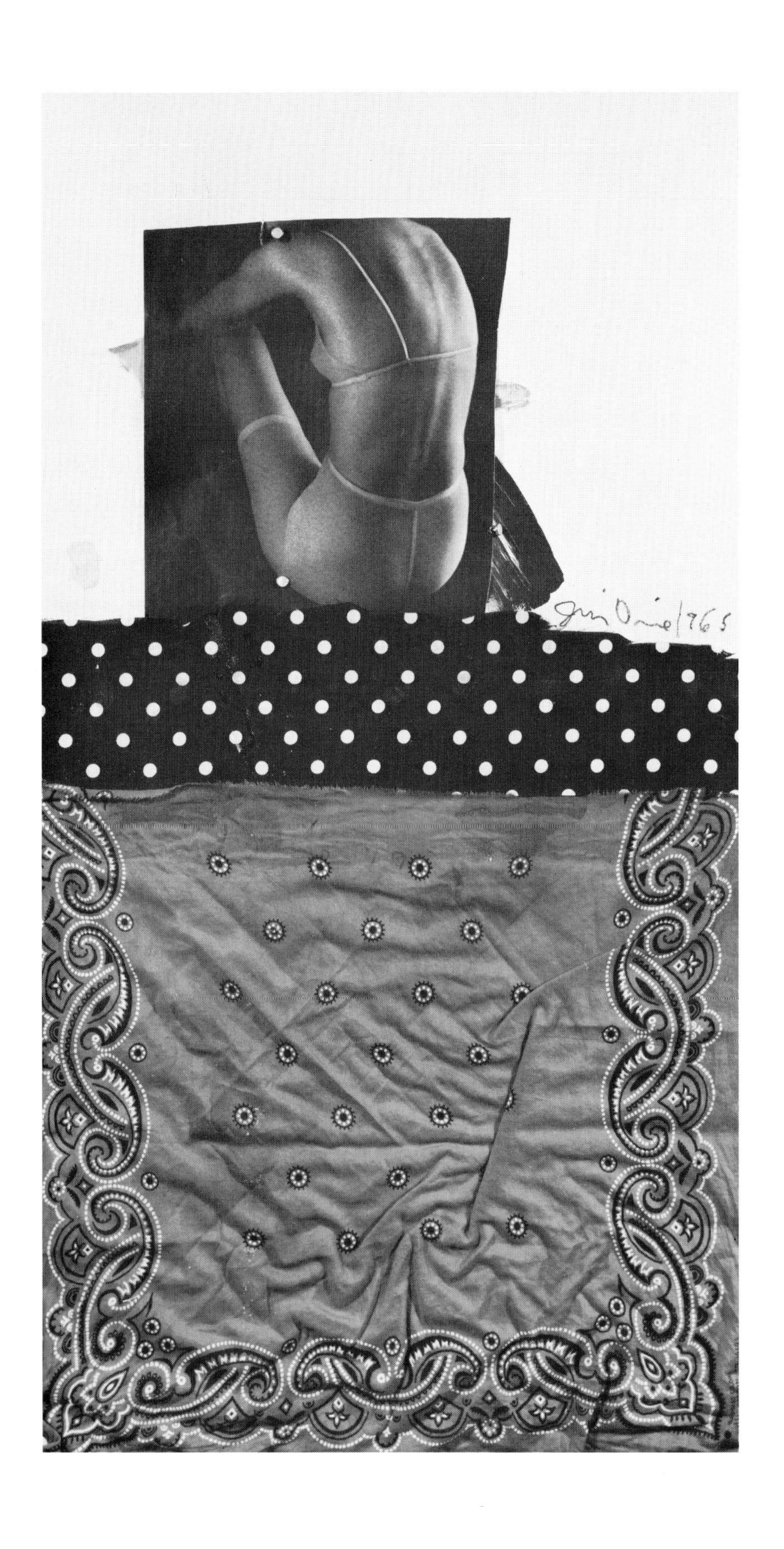

soft drain CO 66

Claes Oldenburg

Born in Stockholm, Sweden, January 28, 1929. New York City, 1929-32.
Oslo, Norway, 1933-36. Chicago, Illinois, 1936-56. B.A. Yale University, 1950.
Apprentice reporter, City News Bureau of Chicago, 1950-51.
Studied at the Art Institute of Chicago, 1953-54. Moved permanently to New York, 1956.
Travels and work outside New York City: Venice, California, August 1963 — April 1964; Paris and Italy, April 1964 — December 1964; Stockholm (for retrospective at Moderna Museet), Oslo and London, August 1966 — December 1966.

Claes Oldenburg

Ellen H. Johnson

In an era when the only constant, from fashion to government to science to philosophy, seems to be change itself, our artists inevitably address themselves to that aspect of reality. Some of them work with actual motion which is a distinctly twentieth-century innovation. Others create plastic metaphors of change in time, a modern tradition which extends at least as far back as Cézanne.

It is this latter domain which Claes Oldenburg explores and extends; and very few artists have made images of mobility and of the process of becoming inherent in life itself with the richness of imagination that he commands. It would be hard to name any of his contemporaries who has had a wider range of ideas and executed them more audaciously than Oldenburg has in the six short years in which he has exhibited and given performances. His happenings are an intrinsic aspect of his object-making. It is not just that they give him ideas for expression in more lasting forms but they reveal the same basic attitude of humility and assertiveness, the same interchange between the given (whether it be materials, objects of his environment or people) and the directed which characterizes all of his work.

Among the particular qualities of Oldenburg's direction are the full-bodied humour, the touching human presence, the sensuousness, the fantasy, the grand scale and intimacy, the ironical inversions, the metamorphoses from one kind of being to another and, above all, the moving, organic character of his images. Drawings, painted reliefs, free-standing objects — all are curiously *alive*. Their life is the life of form, form in relation to human experience. Even though he says he wants "to create an independent object which has its existence in a world outside of both the real world as we know it and the world of art", his fundamental aim, or in any case his achievement, is linked to the tradition of art. How different is Oldenburg's saying "American commercial art with its passionate distance is in a way a model of the 'objective expressionism' I practice" from Baudelaire's "Delacroix was passionately in love with passion and coldly determined to find means of expressing it as clearly as possible"; or how different is Oldenburg's attitude from the cool modernity of Manet? To suggest analogies with the past is certainly not to discount the fantasy, newness, or the "otherness" of Oldenburg's inventions but only to aver that his work *is* art, a realm of created existence flexible enough to allow continuous modification and expansion of its boundaries.

Already in his first exhibited work Oldenburg's power to modify and expand the boundaries of art was unmistakable. His *Céline, Backwards* (no. 25) and *Empire Papa Ray Gun* (no. 26) of 1959 and the burlap pieces, such as *Street Head* (no. 27) of 1960, although owing something to Dubuffet and popular public drawing, were shockingly new images, *constructed* of, not just representing or incorporating, the poignant waste of our urban culture. The dirty old grey, black and brown newspapers and rags, as they evoke the impermanent, restless "reality" of the street, are not unrelated in content to Daumier's more explicit images of humanity on the move. The word Ray Gun was used as the title of an exhibition which he and Dine held at the Judson Gallery in 1960, Oldenburg showing *The Street* and Dine *The House*. This exhibition concluded with a series of happenings by Oldenburg (*Snapshots from the City*), Dine (*The Smiling Workman*), Kaprow, Whitman, Grooms, Hansen, and Higgins. The word Ray Gun was also used for group "comics" or "poems" at that time. In 1962 Oldenburg called a series of performances that he produced The Ray Gun Theatre and his studio became The Ray Gun Manufacturing Company. The Ray Gun image itself is a personal and, as he says, "mystic" one for Oldenburg; but whatever its private significance may be to him, it is an open image of the male, life-giving principle, and the Ray Gun's straightforward, right-angled, strong-armed shape has often appeared in his work.

Oldenburg has referred to *The Street* as "reality" and to *The Store*, which followed it, as "a kind of dream". In 1961 he transformed his studio into a store filled with the results of his fantasy at work on the facts of commercial products and advertising; food, clothing and appliances constructed of chicken-wire, plaster and brilliantly coloured enamel paint. In *Girls' Dresses* (no. 28) and *Oranges Advertisement* (no. 29), from that exhibition, he has allowed the wire to give its mobility to the plaster so that the very ground for the painting shifts and fluctuates like its rapidly changing colour and line.

Not only the reliefs but even the free-standing objects were closer to painting than to sculpture until about the middle of 1962 when the objects became more consciously masses making insistent demands on space. The *Giant Hamburger* (no. 30) and *Giant Ice Cream Cone*, included in his fall 1962 show at the Green Gallery, are among the first works in the new direction. It is characteristic of the plunging boldness of Oldenburg's vision that his first real sculptures are colossal forms whose softness introduces not only the illusion but the actuality of changing form. The pertinent question at that time was not, as the public and many critics believe, "Who ever heard of a seven-foot hamburger?" but rather "Who ever heard of a soft sculpture?" Who ever heard of making sculpture, in fact sewing it, of canvas and foam rubber? (Such ready-mades as Duchamp's historic typewriter cover are objects *found*, not invented and constructed by the artist.) Also, in these decisive works Oldenburg appears to have begun to objectify his experience more, that is, to have gotten more firmly outside of it — but no less involved with it.

Oldenburg's iconography is centered in the street, the store and the home; the latter first appeared as an exclusive theme in his *Bedroom Ensemble* at the Sidney Janis Gallery *4 Environments*, January, 1964, and it dominated his one-man show, at the same gallery in the spring of that year, with its wall-switches and *Outlet with Plug* (no. 32), ironing board, soft telephone (his first vinyl piece), toaster, typewriter and food stuffs (the home and the store and even the street interweave). The October 1964 exhibition at the Ileana Sonnabend Gallery was thematically and visually based on the street-store *charcuteries* and *patisseries* of Paris. Extraordinarily sensitive as Oldenburg is to his environment, when he went over to Paris to prepare an exhibition, inevitably he gave it a different character from the New York or Los Angeles shows. The watercolour *Banana Split # 2 (Paris)* (no. 42) is representative of that French quality in the delicate colours modelling fluid volumes. Cézanne is not far away from this little drawing which is so characteristic of Oldenburg's mixture of grace and strength.

Oldenburg's representation at the Venice Biennale in 1964 and to a considerable extent his Stockholm retrospective in the fall of 1966 (although he did go there prior to the exhibition and contributed directly to it), the subsequent London showing and the present exhibition differ from his one-man gallery shows in that he constructs each of the latter *as* a show, a unit as flexibly controlled as the individual items within it. The thematic and formal coherence of his exhibitions reflects his ability to compose a multitude of elements on a large scale in relation to the spaces of the gallery. The gallery shows of today, when the artist controls them as conclusively as Oldenburg does, are in this regard somewhat like the fresco cycles of differently oriented cultures.

The major motif of his 1966 exhibition at the Janis Gallery was the bathroom, with the new Airflow subject as a subsidiary theme — soft engines, tires, radiators etc. based on various models of a 1930's Chrysler design. Aesthetically, the show was a synthesis of sensuous, flowing forms accentuated by a few crisp, rectangular accents. A variety of materials was harmonized: vinyl, formica, kapok, corrugated cardboard and canvas; surfaces ranged from the highest gloss to the dullest matte. The colors were elegantly refined: brilliant white and black with sudden notes of red and blue combined with the more muted whites of the ghost and hard models and the greys and browns of the city maps and Airflow pieces.

The content of the show (to use Goethe's division of subject, content and form) was no less multiple and complex. Opulence and austerity, abandon and restraint, humour, irony, movement, unfixity, the process of becoming, openness — these are some of the things Oldenburg's art means. All are present in the *Bathtub* series. The contradiction of a hard, rigid tub in soft, giving vinyl and the transformation of such a utilitarian object into something so conspicuously useless are characteristic of his wit. The patent vinyl of *Soft Tub* (no. 38) is shiny and reflective like the porcelain enamel of the actual tub and the invented tub's form flows and changes like water. It looks like a tub, but it also looks like other things, sexual, organic and relaxed. The metamorphosis of details is immediately engaging: the faucets become plane-propellers, the stopper and chain an umbilical cord. However, beyond all the possible associations, its ultimate identity is a boisterously rich, monumental and voluptuous form. As it moves and falls differently in space, inviting and impelling touch and change, it is a marvelously inventive and a beautiful object. The *Ghost Tub (Canvas)* (no. 37) is quieter and somewhat less sensuous; although it is also flexible, its form sometimes takes more angular, harsher folds. It is a more difficult work and it is more drawn into itself, more mysterious, even terrifying. The *Tub (Hard Model)* (no. 36) is as aristocratic and aloof as the Pharaoh whose mummy-case it so obviously resembles. By lightly brushing white paint over brown corrugated paper he creates a subtle, dusty gold colour which adds to the tone of ancient solemnity. Oldenburg has transformed the model of a bathtub into an awesome object. Technically, he makes the hard models first as a quick working-out of the formal idea. In the ghost models he explores the possibility of creating fluid volumes through sewing; in this, the sewing stage of the process, he is assisted by others, particularly his wife Pat who works very closely with him. The vinyl is the final work, but each of the models has its own character, just as in traditional sculpture the plaster and final bronze or marble differ from each other. Oldenburg is in many ways a traditional artist and he is a fine craftsman.

While he might also be considered traditional in that his sculptures deal with subject matter, his materials and the form and scale into which he works them, the subjects he chooses and the multiple, ambiguous identities he gives to them — as he says, "halfway between the real world and the world of art" — are distinctly modern. He rejects the human form of traditional sculpture, but his objects powerfully imply and evoke the human presence. His subjects are the simple, manufactured things which we act intimately upon, in, and with every day. By isolating and fixedly scrutinizing the ordinary objects which we take for granted, he penetrates to their essential form and imbues them with a mysterious power. By giving these things actual three-dimensional existence he makes them more real and at the same time more enigmatic. As Gide wrote of the novelist Céline, "It is not reality which he paints but the hallucinations which reality provokes." This may partly account for the fact that Oldenburg's choice of subject matter does not always, as one might think it should, make his work more accessible to Everyman whom he clearly would like to reach. For some people it does, for others it makes it more difficult than abstract art. Some people bang their heads metaphorically speaking so hard against "bathtub", for example, that they cannot see what they are looking at. But for other people, many of whom simply accept abstract compositions as art and thus take them for granted instead of examining them, Oldenburg's objects make uncomfortable, but rewarding, demands. The shock of a huge soft tub or hamburger catches the observer and forces him to see the difference between it and an ordinary hamburger or tub – and that difference is Oldenburg's art.

25 *Céline, Backwards.* 1959.
Newspaper in wheat paste over wire frame, painted with casein, 32 x 40 in.
Collection the artist.

26 *Empire Papa Ray Gun.* 1959.
Newspaper in wheat paste over wire frame, painted with casein, 39 x 40 in.
Collection the artist.

27 *Street Head.* 1960.
Painted burlap stuffed with paper, approximately 74 x 49 in.
Sidney Janis Gallery

28 *Girls' Dresses.* 1961.
Enamel paint on plaster,
43½ x 41 x 6⅞ in.
Mrs Claes Oldenburg.

29 *Oranges Advertisement.* 1961.
Enamel paint on plaster.
44 x 36½ x 6 in.
Ellen H. Johnson.

30 *Giant Hamburger.* 1962.
Painted sailcloth stuffed with foam rubber, approximately 52 x 84 in.
Sidney Janis Gallery.

31 *Ice Cream Soda with Cookie.* 1963.
Enamel paint on plaster and glass,
11½ x 13¾ x 10¼ in.
Dr and Mrs Sydney L. Wax.

32 *Outlet with Plug.* 1964.
Painted wood, 48½ x 29 x 17 in.
Mr and Mrs Richard Solomon.

33 *Glace en Dégustation.* 1964
Painted plaster and porcelain,
3⅜ x 5⅝ x 9¾ in.
Albright-Knox Art Gallery, Buffalo, gift of Seymour H. Knox.

34 *Model (Ghost) Juicit (Silex Juicit).* 1965.
Wood, liquitex on canvas stuffed with kapok,
19 x 18 x 16 in.
Mr and Mrs Roger Davidson.

35 *Soft Engine Parts #1, Air Flow Model #6 (Radiator and Fan).* 1965.
Wood, stenciled canvas stuffed with kapok, 32 x 24 x 18 in.
Mr and Mrs Marvin Goodman.

36 *Tub (Hard Model).* 1966.
Corrugated paper, enamel and wood,
80 x 32½ x 27½
Sidney Janis Gallery.

37 *Ghost Tub (Canvas).* 1966.
Wood, liquitex on canvas stuffed with foam rubber, 80 x 30 x 30 in.
Dr and Mrs Sydney L. Wax.

38 *Soft Tub.* 1966.
Wood, vinyl stuffed with foam rubber,
80 x 30 x 30 in.
Mr and Mrs Roger Davidson.

39 *Soft Manhattan #1, Postal Zones.* 1966.
Stenciled canvas stuffed with kapok,
80 x 30 x 8 in.
Albright-Knox Art Gallery, Buffalo, gift of Seymour H. Knox.

DRAWINGS

40 *Study for Zebra Chair.* 1963.
Chalk and watercolour on black paper,
26½ x 41 in.
Sidney Janis Gallery.

41 *Plan for Wall Switches.* 1964.
Ink on paper, 28⅝ x 23⅜ in.
Whitney Museum of American Art, New York City,
Neysa McMein Purchase Award.

42 *Banana Split #2 (Paris).* 1964.
Chalk and watercolour on paper,
12¼ x 17½ in.
Allen Memorial Art Museum, Oberlin College, Oberlin.

43 *Colossal Monument for Lower East Side: Ironing Board.* 1965.
Crayon and wash on paper,
21½ x 29¾ in.
Mr and Mrs Marvin Goodman.

44 *Proposed Colossal Monument for Columbus Circle, Silex Juicit in Place of Huntington Hartford Museum.* 1965.
Crayon and wash on paper,
29½ x 21½ in.
Sidney Janis Gallery.

45 *Soft N.Y.* 1965.
Pencil, crayon and wash on paper,
16¾ x 14 in.
Sidney Janis Gallery.

46 *Air Flow Car Study #1.* 1966.
Collage of drawings, 22 x 29¾ in.
Harry N. Abrams Family Collection.

47 *Drain Pipe (T).* 1966.
Crayon and wash on paper,
18³⁄₁₆ x 15 in.
Sidney Janis Gallery.

Céline, Backwards
1959
Newspaper in wheat paste over wire frame,
painted with casein, 32 x 40 in.
Collection the artist

Empire Papa Ray Gun
1959 Newspaper in wheat paste over wire frame,
painted with casein, 39 x 40 in.
Collection the artist

The Ray Guns are unorthodox and unguaranteed talismans . . .
made of the material of a certain time and place
for purposes of protection, inspiration and evocation . . .
They are mounted as relics after their use.

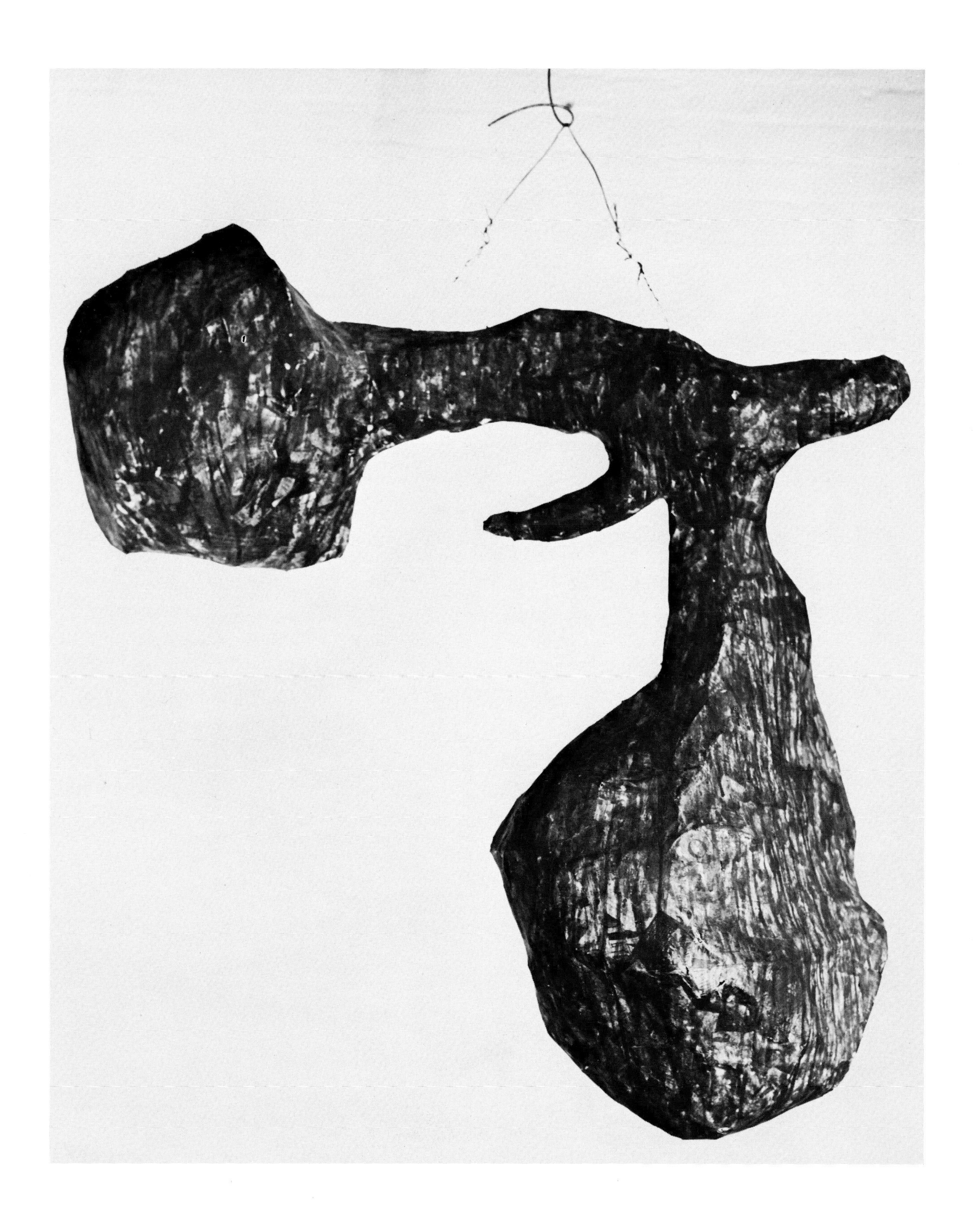

Street Head
1960 Painted burlap stuffed with paper,
approximately 74 x 49 in.
Sidney Janis Gallery

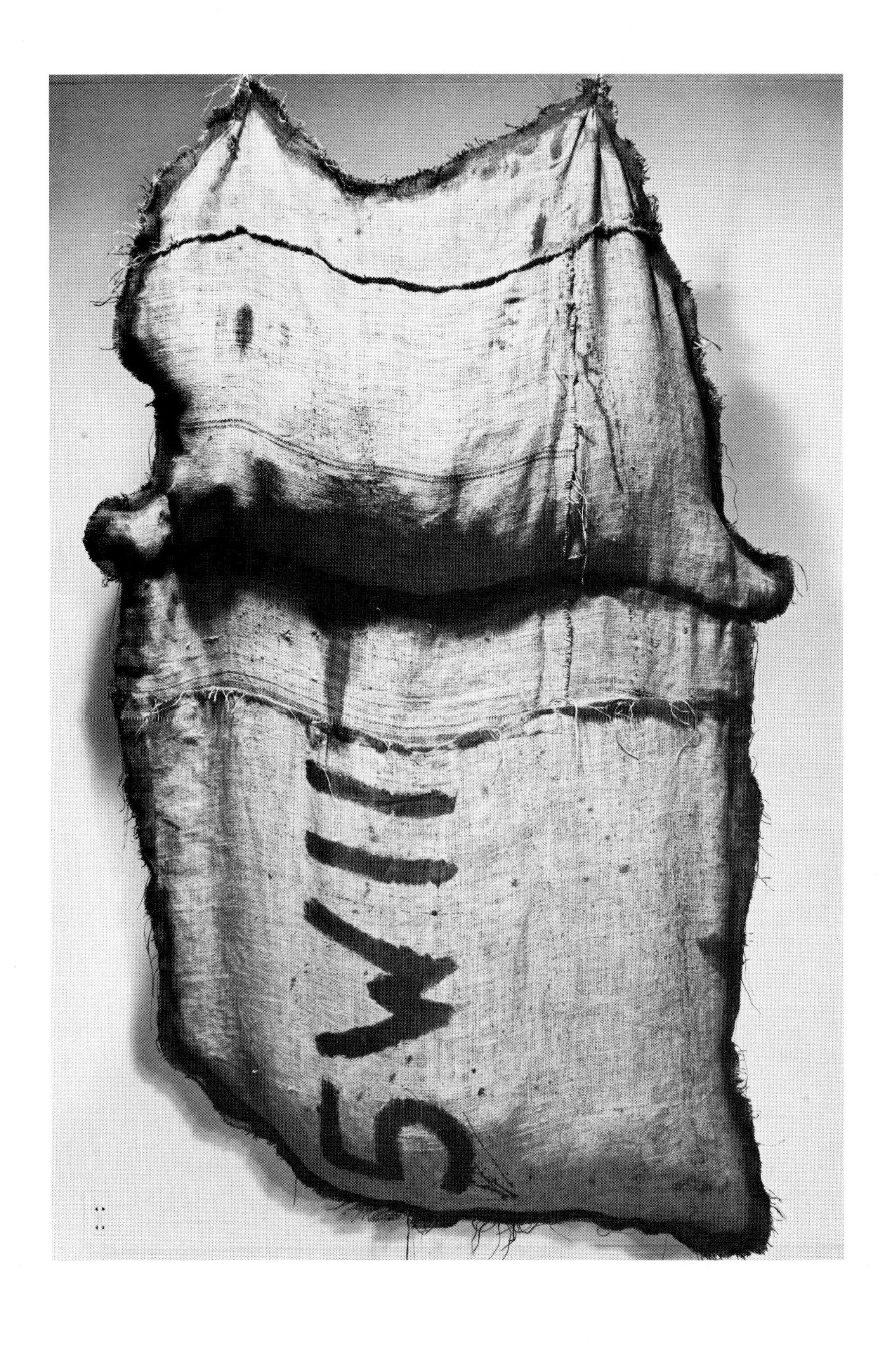

Girl's Dresses
1961
Enamel paint on plaster,
43½ x 41 x 6⅞ in.
Mrs Claes Oldenburg

Oranges Advertisement
1961
Enamel paint on plaster
44 x 36½ x 6 in.
Ellen H. Johnson

Giant Hamburger
1962 Painted sailcloth stuffed with foam rubber, approximately 52 x 84 in.
Sidney Janis Gallery

Some people say,
"This is not art; this is a hamburger."
Other people say, "This is not a hamburger; it is art."

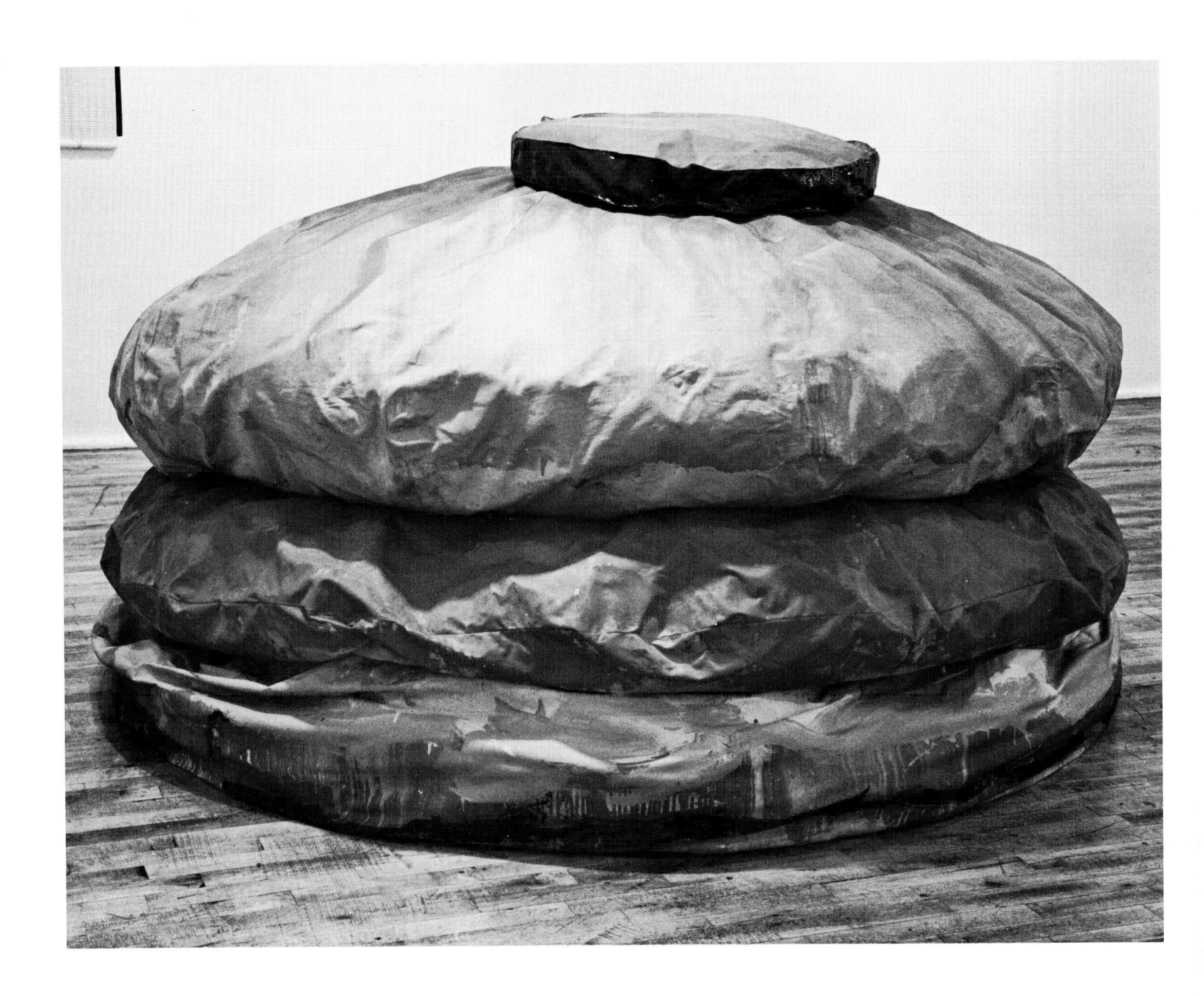

Outlet with Plug
1964 Painted wood, 48½ x 29 x 17 in.
Mr and Mrs Richard Solomon

Ice Cream Soda with Cookie
1963 Enamel paint on plaster and glass,
11½ x 13¾ x 10¼ in.
Dr and Mrs Sydney L. Wax

Glace en Dégustation
1964 Painted plaster and porcelain,
3⅜ x 5⅝ x 9¾ in.
Albright-Knox Art Gallery, Buffalo,
gift of Seymour H. Knox

I made Glace en Dégustation *in Paris.*
Its colours and surface are the result of inhaling
the Parisian scene in the fall of 1964.
It has the fanshaped cracker characteristic
of ice cream served there.

Model (Ghost) Juicit (Silex Juicit)
1965 Wood, liquitex on canvas stuffed with kapok,
19 x 18 x 16 in.
Mr and Mrs Roger Davidson

Everything I do is completely original —
I made it up when I was a little kid.

Soft Engine Parts #1, Air Flow Model #6 (Radiator and Fan)
1965 Wood, stenciled canvas stuffed with kapok,
32 x 24 x 18 in.
Mr and Mrs Marvin Goodman

I am a technological liar.

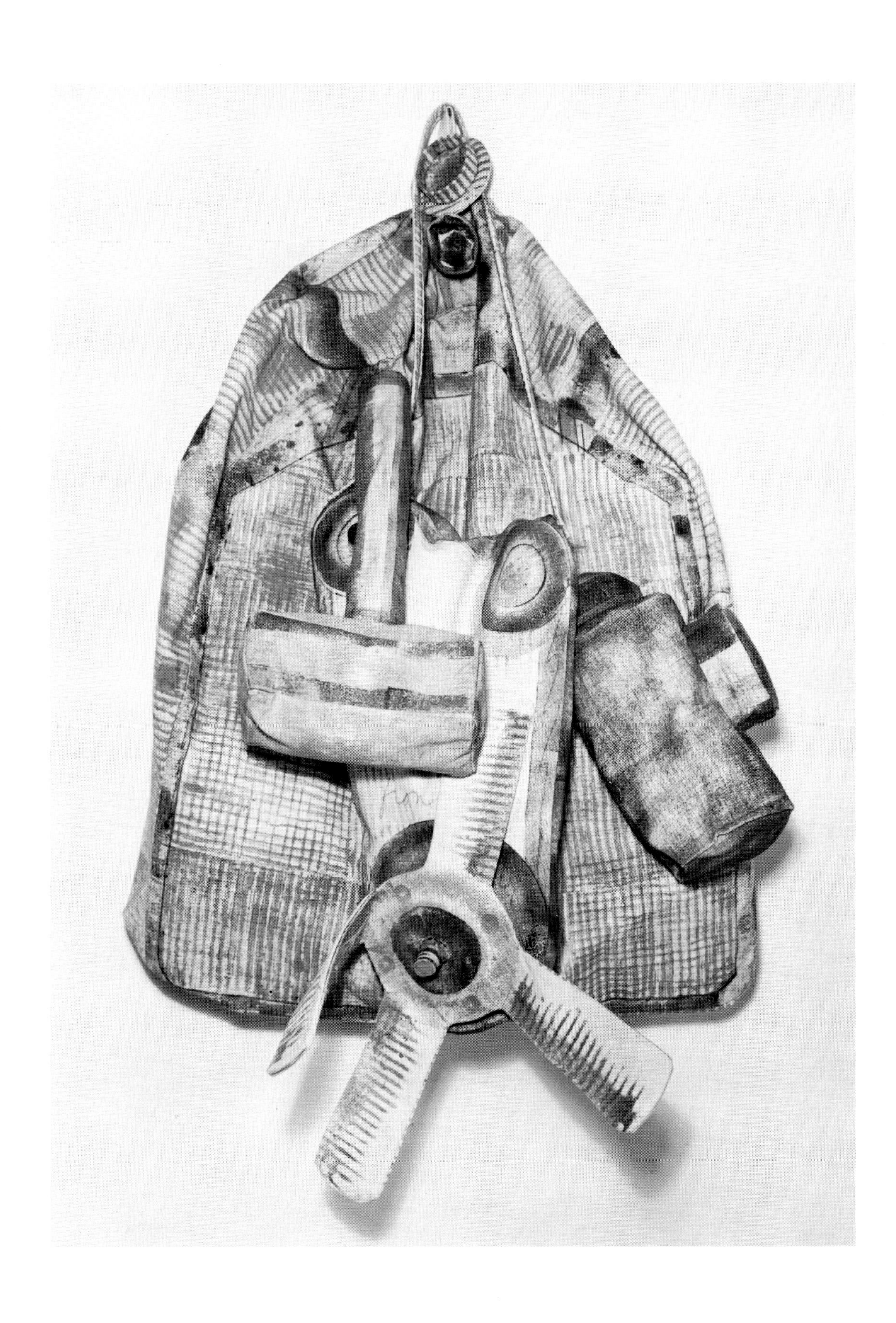

I decide the scale and appearance
of the object and build a model.
From this model I make stencils
and transfer them to material
and cut them for sewing.
After the sewing I stuff the pieces.
I choose the kind of stuffing
and how much and where it will
gather — fat or lean.
This is my "modelling".

Tub (Hard Model)
1966
Corrugated paper,
enamel and wood,
80 x 32½ x 27½ in.
Sidney Janis Gallery
OPPOSITE

Ghost Tub (Canvas)
1966
Wood, liquitex on canvas
stuffed with foam rubber,
80 x 30 x 30 in.
Dr and Mrs Sydney L. Wax

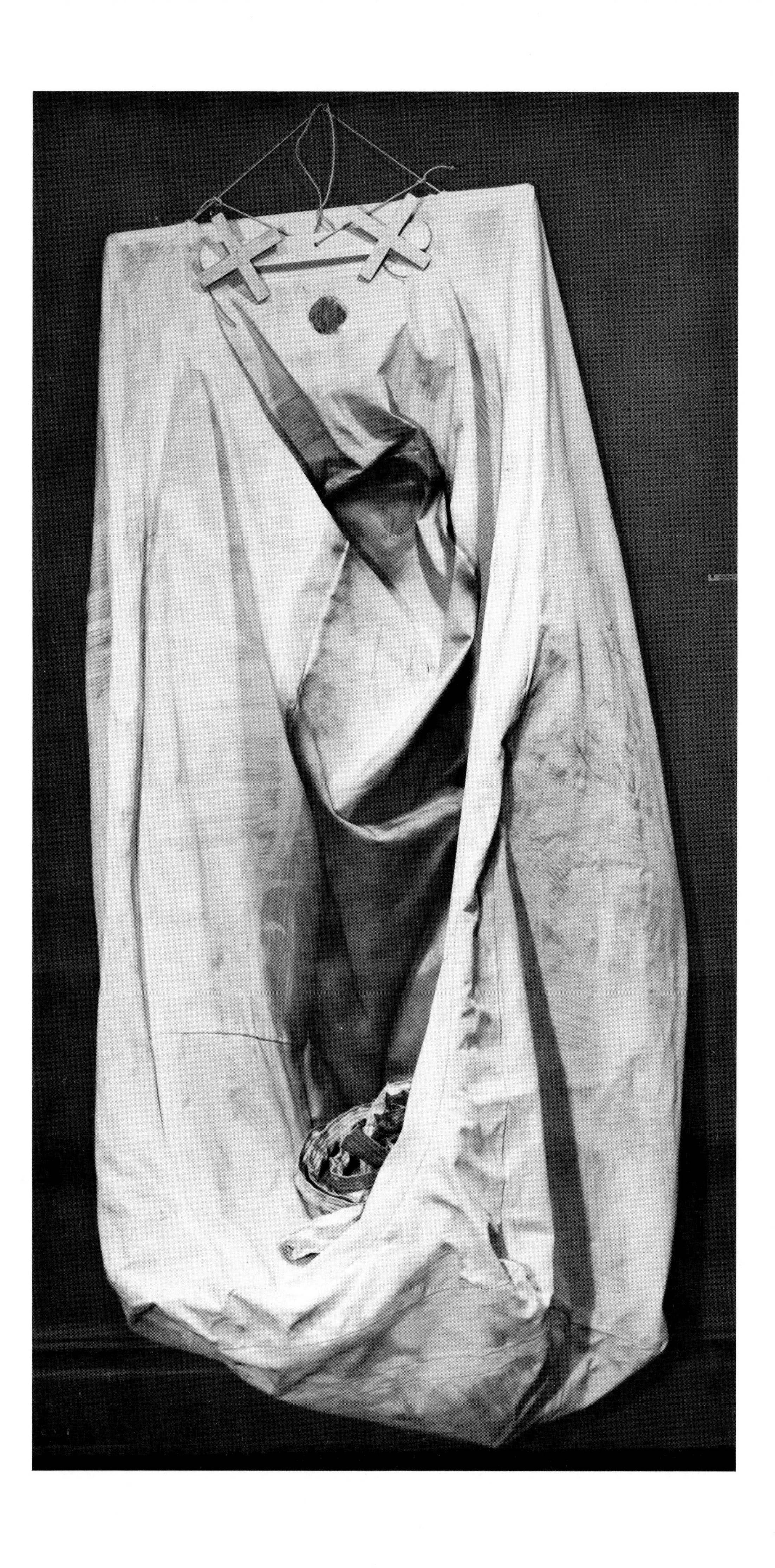

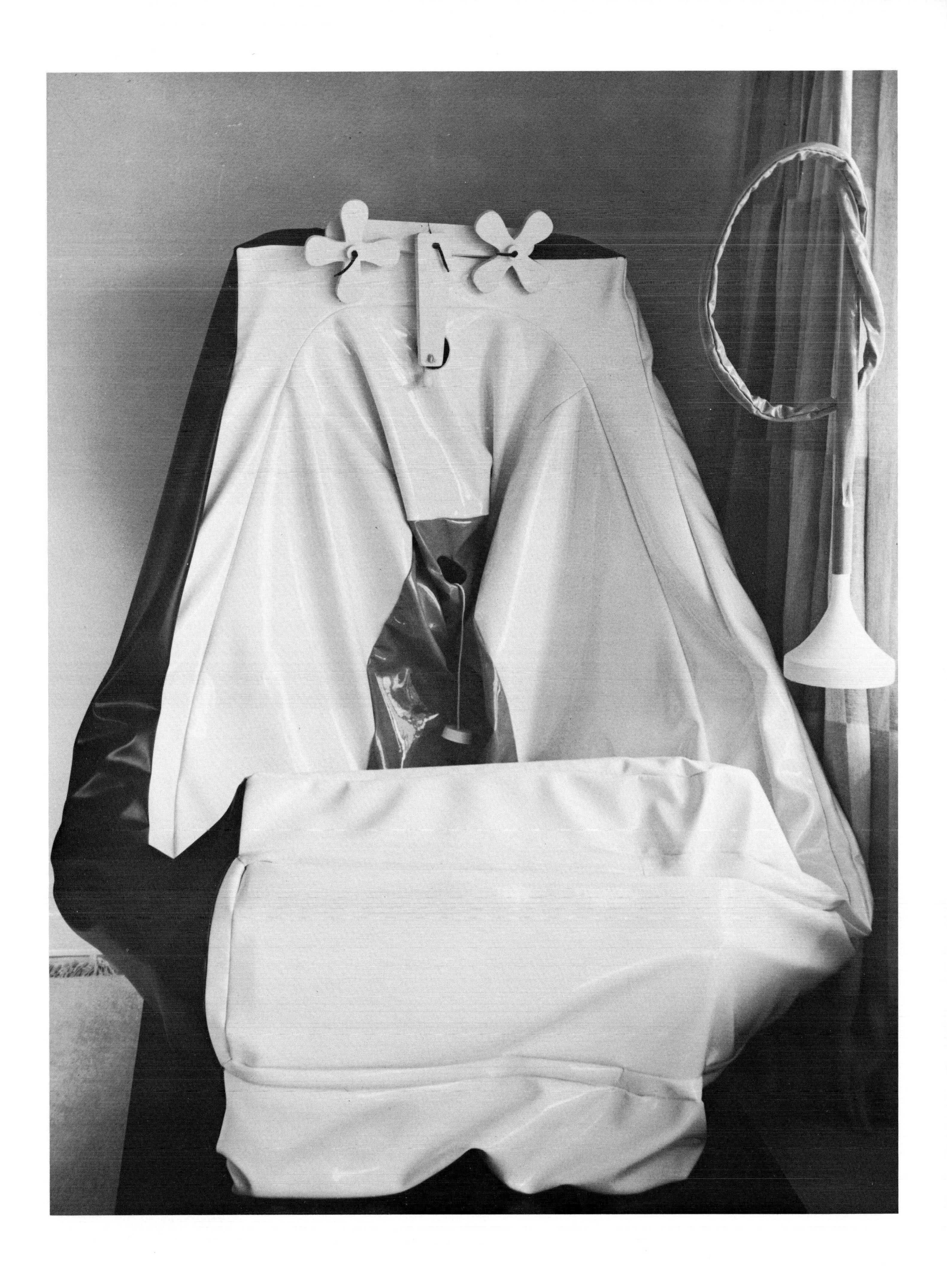

Soft Tub
1966
Wood, vinyl stuffed
with foam rubber,
80 x 30 x 30 in.
Mr and Mrs Roger Davidson
OPPOSITE

Soft Manhattan #1
Postal Zones
1966
Stenciled canvas stuffed
with kapok, 80 x 30 x 8 in.
Albright-Knox Art Gallery,
Buffalo,
gift of Seymour H. Knox

I notice that every time
Manhattan is represented
it is represented differently
— like ancient maps.

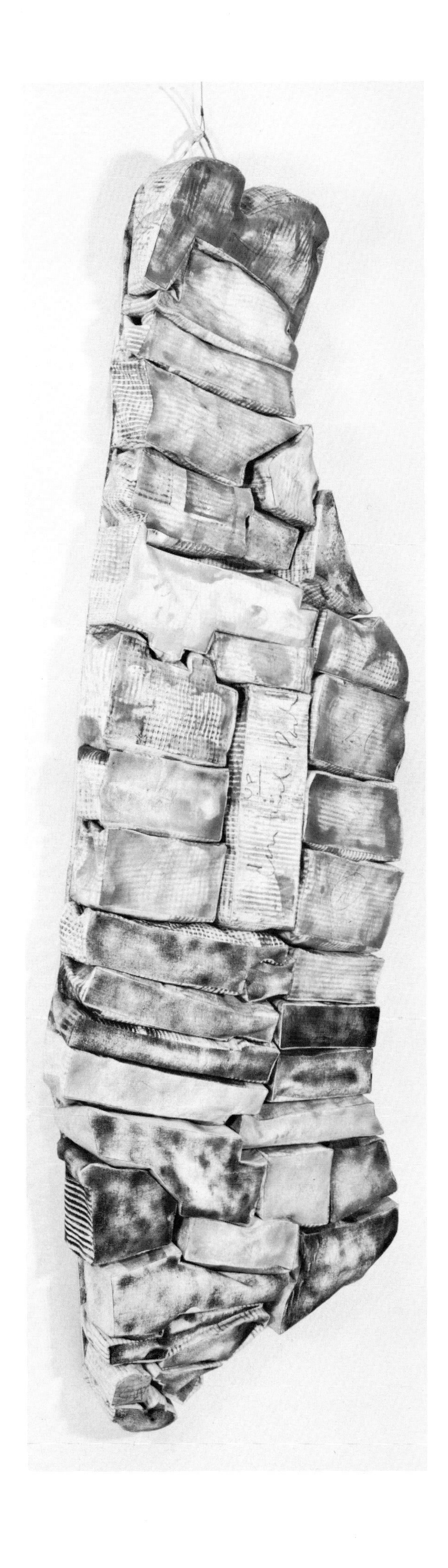

Proposed Colossal Monument for Columbus Circle,
Silex Juicit in Place of Huntington Hartford Museum. 1965
Crayon and wash on paper, 29½ x 21½ in. Sidney Janis Gallery

Colossal Monuments: in which an object from The Street,
The Store or The Home is magnified and set into
appropriate locations in the New York landscape.

DRIVER LICENSE NUMBER
S2215 27800 11242
STATE OF NEW JERSEY
DIVISION OF MOTOR VEHICLES
DRIVER LICENSE
EXPIRATION DATE
FEB 28 67
ISSUE DATE
JAN 24 64
GEORGE SEGAL
RFD4 DAVIDSONMILL
NEW BRUNSWICK N.J.
MO. YEAR
FT. INCHES RESTRICTIONS
1124 2 M 4 2 508 01 8.00
BIRTH DATE EYES SEX WT. HAIR HEIGHT IF ANY FEE
SIGN HERE X George Segal
LS-147A (3-63)
Ned J. Parsekian
DIRECTOR
CARDS

George Segal

Born in New York City, November 26, 1924.
B.A. New York University, 1950. M.F.A. Rutgers University, 1963.
Presently lives in North Brunswick, New Jersey.

George Segal

Robert Pincus-Witten

George Segal is one of the best-known sculptors in the world. His work is included in important public and private collections, and there is scarcely an exhibition of reputation in which he has not been represented. Even certain details of his personal life are familiar to students of contemporary art: that he lives in the country, North Brunswick, New Jersey, on a deactivated chicken farm.

These banalities are repeated in the manner of a nineteenth-century memoir not to remind the reader that it has been a long hard climb to celebrity, but because of their touching irony. George Segal first wanted to be a painter, and, could he have had his choice, preferably Matisse. Certain sculptural qualities in Segal's present work can be retraced to this earlier love.

Although armed with a degree in art education earned at the downtown campus of New York University, Segal quit the city and decided to give his life an economic focus by running a chicken farm while beginning his career as an artist. Being close to the Rutgers University campus, he encountered one day a young faculty member, Allan Kaprow, through whom Segal was exposed, first-hand, to the students and the teaching practice of Hans Hoffman (although Hoffman's principles were then the current methodology and were as accessible outside of the master's studio as in it). Like many young artists of the immediately postwar generation emancipated by Abstract Expressionism, Segal's painting at the time revealed a primitive sense of colour and paint manipulation, nonchalant drawing, an anchored composition and, somewhat unusually, a fundamental reliance on the imagery of the human figure. His models were Matisse and, in a less-obvious way, Bonnard. In short, Segal wanted to be a great French painter.

Ten years ago, Segal had his first one-man show at the old Hansa Gallery, a cooperative venture co-directed by Richard Bellamy and Ivan Karp, which included, among others, Allan Kaprow, Jan Müller, Richard Stankiewicz and Wolf Kahn, artists, at the time, of Hoffmanesque and representational dispositions. Segal's exhibition was received indifferently. Here was still another young painter in the train of Matisse attempting to find himself: "He leads off with bright, primary colors which, for no explainable reason, became muddied. . . . But here again there is a muddy corner as if all the problems of the painting had placed themselves in one, untidy heap."[1]

Parker Tyler recognized hints of Bonnard's light, Matisse's drawing and flat Japanese patterns.[2] In May 1957, at the time of the second exhibition at the Hansa Gallery, Tyler was still dubious of Segal's "re-evocation of Bonnard's solarization. . . . One can fairly taste the palette-saturation." He grudgingly admitted that Segal's *"goût* for color and surface texture is already an accomplished thing."[3] Matisse and Bonnard were again cited, as well as Degas and Lautrec, in reference to Segal's pastels.

In February 1958, in connection with the third show, the reviews began to lose some of their reserve. John Ashbury saw Segal's pictures as "un-morbid Expressionist paintings of nudes in country interiors. . . . The figures are powerfully situated in space... the palette is sensuous and acrid (mauve-red-mahogany); the pigment juicy, worked up in a fine yet calculating frenzy: behind their surface turbulence these paintings have a cool detachment."[4]

During 1958, Segal first realized the possibility of a sculptural rather than a painterly solution and experimented with life-scale figures. Compared to his present technical command, these early attempts were impulsive and awkward. Three such sculptures were included in Segal's fourth exhibition at the Hansa Gallery. Neither portraits nor casts after his friends, they were "life-size figures [made] out of wire, plaster and burlap, one sitting, one standing and one lying. They looked to me as if they had stepped out of my paintings."[5]

James Schuyler and Sidney Tillim were struck by this unanticipated change in media. Referring to the

1/B. G. [Barbara Guest]. "George Segal", exhibition review, *Arts*, March 1956, pp. 60-61.
2/P. T. [Parker Tyler]. "George Segal", exhibition review, *Art News*, March 1956, p. 58.
3/P. T. [Parker Tyler]. "George Segal", exhibition review, *Art News*, May 1957, p. 12.
4/J. A. [John Ashbury]. "George Segal", exhibition review, *Art News*, February 1958, p. 11.
5/Henry Geldzahler. "An Interview with George Segal", *Artforum*, November 1964, p. 26.

figures, Schuyler acknowledged that "Their effect is of a swiftly improvised immediacy, with the arrested movement of a Pompeian dog. Which is not as morbid as it sounds: rather, it is an expression of the urgency of their energy."[6] The paintings, especially the more finished works, Schuyler judiciously observed, were carried "beyond the duration of what inspires his imagination."

"The distance between Segal's drawing and his sculpture" wrote Tillim "is less a measure of his competency than a comment on the function of technique in his style. His paintings, falling somewhere between the two, only confirm an impression of a particularly knotty conflict between freedom and limitation that looks to physical means for a solution." Not that Tillim was especially delighted by the tangible results of this dialectical struggle. He found the three sculptured figures to be "outright grotesques, with parts of the armature visibly adding to the effect. Segal's failure here to come to grips with his medium implies the expediency that in varying degrees is responsible for the reckless excitement to which he too readily surrenders his ideas."[7]

There can be little question that these first sculptural attempts were highly coloured by the prevailing Abstract Expressionist modes, and that, for Segal, the messiness and rudimentary conception of his figures paralleled the battlefield into which the Abstract Expressionist painter had transformed his canvas. As recently as December 1965, Dore Ashton could write that Segal's "use of lumpy, ill-defined details resembles the blurring and erasures that began to cover up a multitude of sins in the works of abstract expressionist epigones."[8]

In November 1960, Segal exhibited at the pioneering Green Gallery directed by Richard Bellamy. He continued to show both paintings and sculptures, which James Beck saw as an amalgam of the German Expressionists and Matisse.[9] In Segal's "interchangeable set of nudes"[10] Tillim observed a derivation from Courbet.

During 1960-61 the second major crisis in Segal's work occurred: the definitive break with painting (although he continued to draw in pastel) and, equally important, the switch from fictitious, figurative sculpture to castings of identifiable personages. These figures, caught in fleeting, simple, human gestures, and placed in architectural indices and para-environments, rank among the most significant sculptural contributions of mid-twentieth-century American art.

In the spring of 1962 a group of eloquent figures were exhibited at the Green Gallery. The consternation they produced was great, and they were widely misinterpreted. It was a moment of general disaffection for Abstract Expressionism, although its fair and dark siblings, Pop Art and reductive art, had not yet fully dawned upon public awareness. For this reason the shocking unfamiliarity of Segal's plaster effigies allied him, for better or worse, with the ascending Pop faction, even though today, four years later, it is clearly evident that Segal's figuration is in no sense symptomatic of the industrial and satirical chauvinism central to Pop ideology. The coincidental parallel between Segal's own evolution as a realistic artist and the development of a larger, figurative movement tended to obscure the fact that Segal had always been a representational artist who was warm and responsive toward life, where others were cold and lampooning.

People felt threatened by Segal's inert plaster figures which contrasted so violently with factual, apparently artless environments. As Marcel Duchamp, however, has written as an introduction to Segal's 1965 exhibition at the Sidney Janis Gallery: "With Segal it's not a matter of the found object; it's the chosen object." The public, unfamiliar with Segal's development, failed to take into account his evolution and the humane impulses which initiated his sculptural work. For, above all else, Segal is a lover, and his work has always closely reflected his personal relationships. From the first, his sculpture has been cast from friends and acquaintances.

"I usually make sculptures of people I know very well," Segal said recently "in situations that I've known them in. And if that involves a luncheonette-counter, places in the house or other places where I go: gas-stations, bus-stations, streets, farm buildings – this must all do with my experience. I live in this environment. . . . It is a huge heap of art material for me. . . . I remember my life with the objects and I also look at these objects 'plastically' (I suppose that is the term), 'esthetically', for what these shapes are. And how people relate to these shapes and how they don't relate in a human way, intrigues me. . . . As long as there has been a very alive emotional experience between me and the person, or between me and the object, or both, only then do I incorporate it into my own work."[11]

Jill Johnson, reviewing Segal's 1962 exhibition, felt that Segal had "made an absurdly real 'environment' for his figures in a room full of plaster people engaged in everyday actions, seated on real chairs at real tables. . . . The charming absurdity of this scene lies in its combination of the artifact with the artifact's 'ready-made' environment – a combination expressing the absurd position some artists find themselves in today."[12] The focus on absurdity has passed, although at the time it was one of the most revealing interpretive guides, based, in part, on transplanted theatrical criticism (applicable to Segal because of the tableau-like character of his groups) and, in part, on the rehabilitation of Marcel Duchamp's oeuvre which occurred at that moment. The reference to "ready-made" is symptomatic.

Allan Kaprow, a director and leading theorist of the Happening movement, very feelingly emphasized the nostalgic, even sentimental, impetus behind Segal's sculpture, at a time when it would have been tempting to perceive them as stills from a Happening. "His works" Kaprow wrote "are, foremost, involvements with his friends with whom he has a specific relationship. By wrapping bandages dipped in wet plaster around the parts of their bodies, cutting off the hardened sections, then later re-assembling them into the whole body, he 'touches' them and possesses them physically and psychically with a contact that would be possible in no other way. Both for him and for us he evokes their presence; they are almost real because they have substance and a name."[13] To my mind this comes as close to stating the real inspiration of Segal's production as any other apposite simile yet devised. ("Pompeian" is the most common.) From this moment on Segal's sculptural notion more or less has set. Each subsequent exhibition has tended to explore some new poignant locus or technical procedure.

Since the early 'sixties a stockpile of Segal exegesis has been taking shape. Two appraisals put forth in 1964 particularly stand out. Kaprow's "Vital Mummies" has already been referred to. Noting the feel of "Old Kingdom statuary", "the detached grandeur of fifteenth-century Italian portraiture" and reminiscences of Pompeii, Kaprow recalled for the reader the scandal surrounding the displaying of Rodin's "Age of Bronze", at which time Rodin had been accused of casting from life, a charge Rodin was at pains to dismiss as vehemently as Segal acknowledges the procedure, with the following exception. "Like mummies . . . the inside of Segal's figures remain true to life in reverse, a fairly exact impression of the skin and clothing of the model, while their outsides tend to be built up, transposed and impersonal, revealing the marks of the artist's hand."[14] The subtle article concludes with an aesthetic conceit: Kaprow imagines a situation in which the figures are real and the objects are turned to plaster. Kaprow contends that the effect would be the same and the vision as profound. It seems to me that only the elements of the art-life dialectic central to pop theory (and disparaged by Kaprow as *"the witty pun"*) have been transposed.

Gene Swenson, in another speculation of interest, asked, "How can arrangements be made which enter experience so vividly that questions of art become irrelevant?" Taking issue with Segal's celebrated *Gas Station,* Swenson hints at a solution to his own conundrum. "It is not that *we* should be able to use the oil or Coke machine; it is that the white plaster service station attendant and truck driver need to be able to use them. Otherwise their propriety and our sense of life are violated."[15]

One thing is evident from these reflections: Segal's work stimulated extremely perplexing intellectual and perceptual problems. Responsible viewers were suddenly challenged by seemingly difficult and indigestible work. "The catatonic presences of George Segal that act concussively upon the environment until it too subsides into something like art"[16] is an attempt by Suzi Gablik to say that one is dealing with a powerful, unfamiliar work which as yet resists art-historical tags, as it still does.

In part, Segal's task has been to replenish an ancient and honourable stream run dry in the mid-twentieth century. Among the more difficult achievements for an artist in our time is to be a realist without falling into anecdote or mere illustration. In terms of his accomplishment Segal is less a relation of Rosenquist, Warhol or Oldenburg, than of Francis Bacon and Edward Hopper. Like Segal, these artists have no bolstering stylistic appellation. Their works are not representative examples of a certain trend. Each piece is judged anew. Each stands or falls on its own communicative merits. For want of a wittier name these artists may be termed Realists.

Now that both the Pop and Optical tendencies are grown hoary, and that, ostensibly, the strongest work being produced today is of a reductive nature, Segal's art remains even more alienated than before. At least during Pop's sway some affiliation between Duchamp's *Bottle Rack* and Segal's Everyman could be argued. To insist upon it today seems to miss the point. Segal is, in an exalted sense, a realist and a stoic. His sober view of human existence does not differ especially from the victims of isolation presented by Hopper, a resemblance observed by both Anne Hoene and me at the time of Segal's most recent one-man show. The sullen and fatigued appearance of the figures led me then to describe them as "metaphors of a vast, inarticulate ordinariness" and to see in Segal "the wholly unanticipated heir of Edward Hopper."[17]

Segal's work falls completely outside the abstract mainstream of twentieth-century art. On the other hand, his work is infinitely more profound and human than that of the general run of Pop artists, whose strength depends less on their existential perception than on their uncanny ability to parody [even through straight-faced exterior imitation] continually new and topical issues. At present Segal nobly occupies an isolated and tenuous position in contemporary art.

6/J. S. [James Schuyler]. "George Segal", exhibition review, *Art News,* February 1959, p. 16.
7/S. T. [Sidney Tillim]. "George Segal", exhibition review, *Arts,* February 1959, pp. 57-58.
8/Dore Ashton. "Life and Movement without Recession", *Studio International*, December 1965, p. 252.
9/J. H. B. [James H. Beck]. "George Segal", exhibition review, *Art News*, November 1960, p. 14.
10/S. T. [Sidney Tillim]. "George Segal", exhibition review, *Arts,* December 1960, p. 54.
11/Jean Dypréau. "Metamorphoses: L'école de New York", *Quadrum XVIII*, 1965, p. 164.
12/J. J. [Jill Johnson]. "George Segal", exhibition review, *Art News*, May 1962, p. 16.
13/Allan Kaprow. "Segal's Vital Mummies", *Art News*, February 1964, p. 33.
14/*Ibid*., p. 33.
15/G. R. S. [Gene R. Swenson]. "George Segal", exhibition review, *Art News*, May 1964, p. 11.
16/Suzi Gablik. "Meta-trompe-l'oeil", *Art News*, March 1965, p. 49.
17/Robert Pincus-Witten. "George Segal", exhibition review, *Artforum*, December 1965, pp. 51-53.

48 *Man Sitting at Table.* 1961.
Plaster and mixed media,
53 x 48 x 48 in.
Sidney Janis Gallery.

49 *Cinema.* 1963.
Plaster and mixed media,
118 x 96 x 39 in.
Albright-Knox Art Gallery, Buffalo,
gift of Seymour H. Knox.
To be shown in Buffalo only.

50 *Couple at the Stairs.* 1964.
Plaster and mixed media,
120 x 104 x 96 in.
Sidney Janis Gallery.

51 *Ruth in the Kitchen.* 1966.
(second version).
Plaster and mixed media,
50 x 72 x 60 in.
Sidney Janis Gallery.

52 *Girl Washing Her Foot.* 1964-65.
Plaster and mixed media,
60 x 28 x 36 in.
Sidney Janis Gallery.

53 *The Butcher Shop.* 1965.
Plaster and mixed media,
94 x 99¼ x 48 in.
Art Gallery of Ontario, Toronto,
gift from Women's Committee Fund, 1966.
To be shown in Toronto only.

54 *The Costume Party.* 1965.
Acrylic on plaster and mixed media,
72 x 144 x 108 in.
Sidney Janis Gallery.

DRAWINGS

55 *Head.* 1964.
Pastel on coloured paper, 18 x 12 in.
Harry N. Abrams Family Collection.

56 *Untitled.* 1964.
Pastel on coloured paper, 18 x 12 in.
Sidney Janis Gallery.

57 *Untitled.* 1965.
Pastel on coloured paper, 18 x 12 in.
Mr and Mrs Marvin Goodman.

58 *Untitled.* 1965.
Pastel on coloured paper, 18 x 12 in.
Sidney Janis Gallery.

59 *Untitled.* 1965.
Pastel on coloured paper, 18 x 12 in.
Sidney Janis Gallery.

60 *Untitled.* 1965.
Pastel on coloured paper, 18 x 12 in.
Sidney Janis Gallery.

Man Sitting at Table
1961
Plaster and mixed media, 53 x 48 x 48 in.
Sidney Janis Gallery

This is the first piece I made using the casting process.
The figure is myself. It ended up a self-portrait with an Egyptian feeling.
I was fascinated by the plastic play of the innumerable legs.

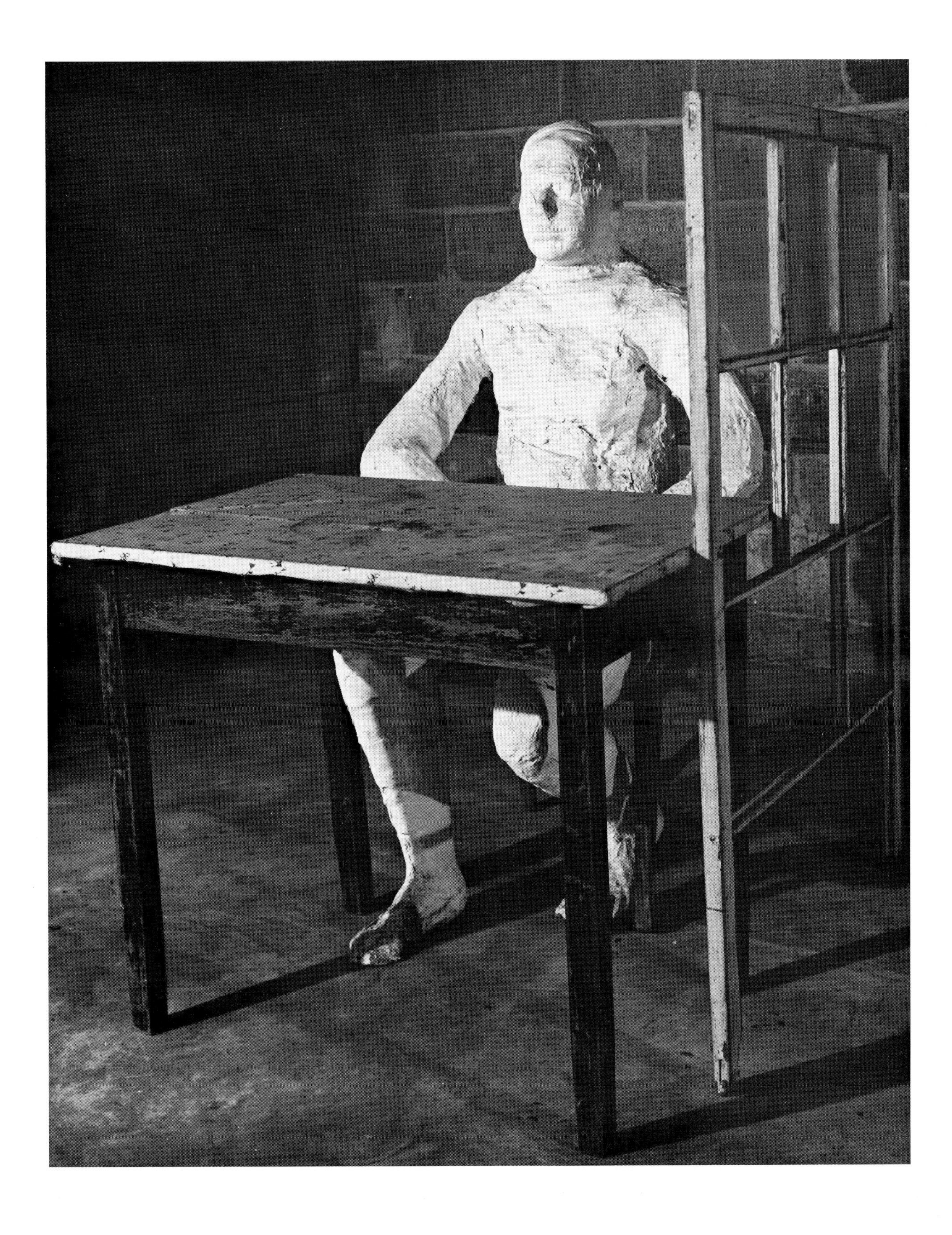

We flashed by the sign at 2:30 in the morning
and I saw the man reaching and said, "look!"
And Helen [Segal's wife] *saw the man crouching.*

Cinema
1963
Plaster and mixed media,
118 x 96 x 39 in.
Albright-Knox Art Gallery,
Buffalo,
gift of Seymour H. Knox
To be shown in Buffalo only

Couple at the Stairs
1964
Plaster and mixed media,
120 x 104 x 96 in.
Sidney Janis Gallery
OPPOSITE

I've been both voyeur and participant in this situation.
I found the stairway in a junkyard, the mailbox in a house being wrecked,
made the ancient wall out of new plywood and paint.
I am still startled when I walk into an old hallway.

Ruth in the Kitchen 1964 (first version)

Ruth in the Kitchen 1966 (second version)
Plaster and mixed media, 50 x 72 x 60 in.
Sidney Janis Gallery

This is the second, stripped-down, version of Ruth in her kitchen.
The original was crammed with a thousand of her own objects.
They decayed. I couldn't stand the mausoleum effect
so I removed them. The whole thing is about Ruth's life, not her tomb.

The girl who posed for this would wash her foot in the sink.
The unexpected thing that happened after the piece was finished was that the gesture reminded me, in a strange way, of Hindu sculpture.

The Butcher Shop
1965
Plaster and mixed media,
94 x 99¼ x 48 in.
Art Gallery of Ontario,
Toronto,
gift from Women's
Committee Fund, 1966
To be shown in
Toronto only
OPPOSITE

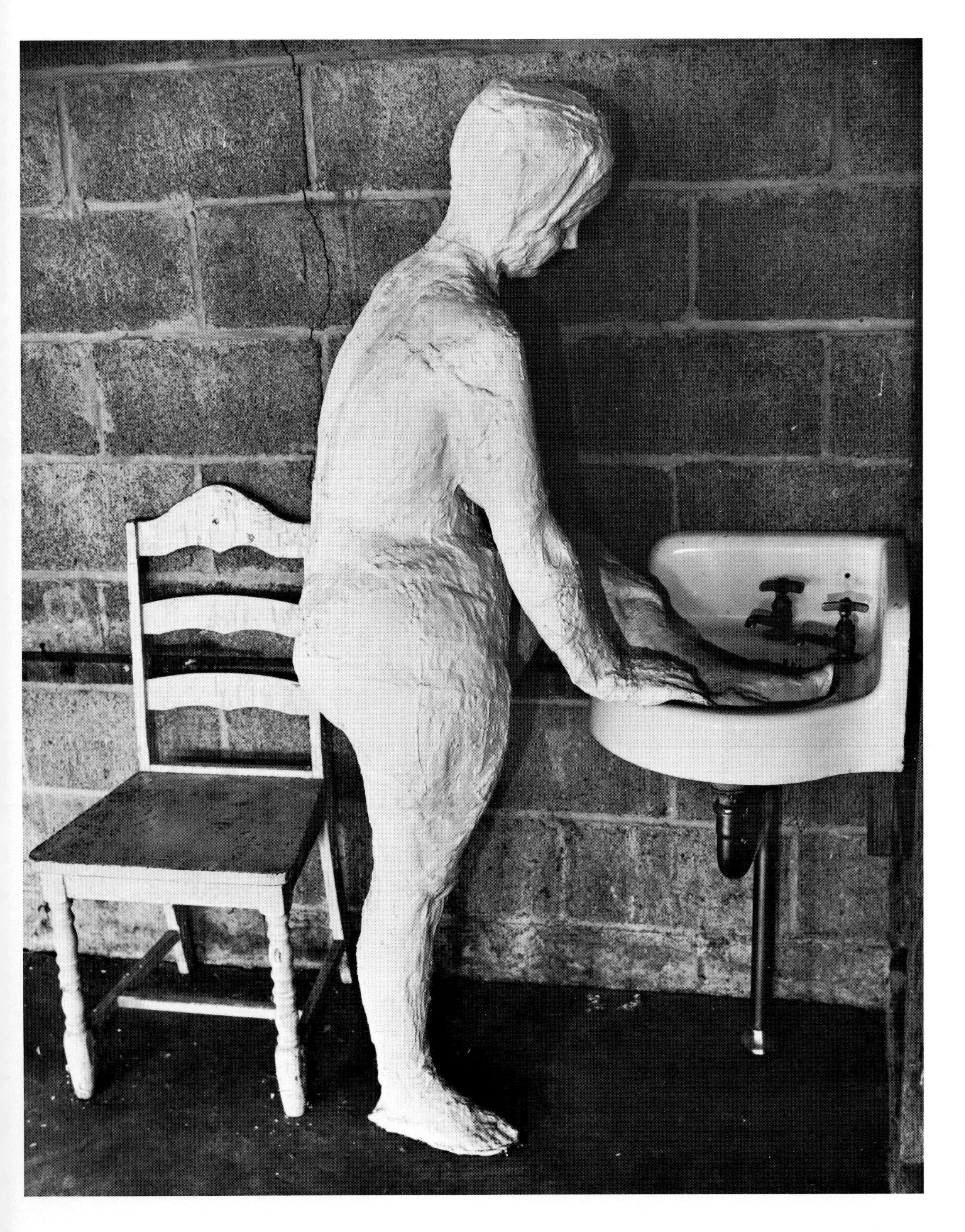

Girl Washing Her Foot
1964-65
Plaster and mixed media,
60 x 28 x 36 in.
Sidney Janis Gallery

This is a requiem for my father. My mother posed.

The Costume Party
1965
Acrylic on plaster and mixed media, 72 x 144 x 108 in.
Sidney Janis Gallery

This is the first time I ever used friends ruthlessly to project my own dark state of mind at the time. The bright colors added somehow to the nightmare qualities of the piece.

Untitled
1965
Pastel on coloured paper, 18 x 12 in.
Mr and Mrs Marvin Goodman

Jim Dine

Lawrence Alloway — 'Apropos of Jim Dine', *Allen Memorial Art Museum Bulletin*, Oberlin College, Fall 1965, pp. 21-27.

'Notes on Five New York Painters', *Albright-Knox Art Gallery Notes*, Autumn 1963, pp. 13-20.

Mario Amaya — *Pop as Art: a Survey of the New Super Realism*, London: Studio Vista, 1965, pp. 78-79.

Cyril Barrett — 'Jim Dine's London', *Studio International*, September 1966, pp. 122-123.

Oyvind Fahlstrom — 'Someone Says: It Really Looks Like It', *New Paintings by Jim Dine* catalogue, Sidney Janis Gallery, New York, February 4 – March 2, 1963.

Robert Fraser — 'Dining with Jim', *Art and Artists*, September 1966, pp. 48-53. (interview with Jim Dine)

Ellen Johnson — 'Jim Dine and Jasper Johns: Art About Art', *Art and Literature*, Autumn 1965, pp. 128-140.

Michael Kirby — *Happenings: An Illustrated Anthology*, New York: E. P. Dutton and Co., Inc., 1965, pp. 184-199. (includes statement by Dine)

Kenneth Koch and Jim Dine — 'Test in Art', *Art News*, October 1966, pp. 54-59.

Max Kozloff — 'The Honest Elusiveness of James Dine', *Artforum*, December 1964, pp. 36-40.

Brydon Smith — 'Jim Dine – Magic and Reality', *Canadian Art*, January 1966, pp. 30-34.

Alan Solomon — 'Jim Dine and the Psychology of the New Art', *Art International*, October 1964, pp. 52-56.
'Four Younger Artists', *XXXII International Biennial Exhibition of Art, United States of America*, Venice, June – October 1964.

G. R. Swenson — 'What is Pop Art', *Art News*, November 1963, p. 24 ff. (includes an interview with Jim Dine)

David Zack — 'A black comedy', *Artforum*, May 1966, pp. 32-34.

Claes Oldenburg

Stockholm 1966 — *Claes Oldenburg, Skulpturer och teckningar*, Moderna Museet, September 17 – October 30. (includes statements in English by Oldenburg)

Mario Amaya — *Pop as Art: a Survey of the New Super Realism*, London: Studio Vista, 1965, pp. 92-93.

Bruce Glaser [moderator] — 'Oldenburg/Lichtenstein/Warhol: A Discussion', *Artforum*, February 1966, pp. 20-24.

Ellen H. Johnson — 'Is Beauty Dead?', *Allen Memorial Art Museum Bulletin*, Oberlin College, Winter 1963, pp. 56-66.

'The Living Object', *Art International*, January 1963, pp. 42-45.

Michael Kirby — *Happenings: An Illustrated Anthology*, New York: E. P. Dutton and Co., Inc., 1965, pp. 200-288. (includes statement by Oldenburg)

Claes Oldenburg — Statement in *Environments, Situations, Spaces* catalogue, Martha Jackson Gallery, New York, May 25 – June 23, 1961.

'Extracts from the Studio Notes 1962-64', *Artforum*, January 1966, pp. 32-33.

'Studio Notes', *New work by Oldenburg* catalogue, Sidney Janis Gallery, New York, March 9 – April 2, 1966.

'The Object: still life', *Craft Horizons*, September/October 1965, pp. 31-32 ff. (interview with Claes Oldenburg)

Harris Rosenstein — 'Climbing Mt. Oldenburg', *Art News*, February 1966, pp. 22-25 ff.

J. Rublowsky — *Pop Art*, New York: Basic Books Inc., 1965, pp. 60-85. (includes brief statements by Oldenburg)

Alan Solomon — 'Four Younger Artists', *XXXII International Biennial Exhibition of Art, United States of America*, Venice, June – October 1964.

Jan van der Marck — 'Claes Oldenburg', *Eight Sculptors: the ambiguous image*, Walker Art Center, Minneapolis, October 22 – December 4, 1966, pp. 14-17.

George Segal

Mario Amaya — *Pop as Art: a Survey of the New Super Realism*, London: Studio Vista, 1965, pp. 97-98.

Ursula Eland — 'George Segal', *Albright-Knox Art Gallery Notes*, Spring 1964, p. 12.

Henry Geldzahler — 'An interview with George Segal', *Artforum*, November 1964, pp. 26-29.

Ellen H. Johnson — 'The Sculpture of George Segal', *Art International*, March 1964, pp. 46-49.

Allan Kaprow — 'Segal's Vital Mummies', *Art News*, February 1964, pp. 30-33 f.

Jan van der Marck — 'George Segal', *Eight Sculptors: the ambiguous image*, Walker Art Center, Minneapolis, October 22 – December 4, 1966, pp. 26-29. (includes brief statements by Segal)

THE CATALOGUE

In the listing of dimensions, height precedes width precedes depth.

The statements by Jim Dine and Claes Oldenburg are taken from previous publications listed in the selected bibliography and correspondence with Brydon Smith. The statements by George Segal were written for this catalogue.

CREDITS

PHOTOGRAPHY

Nancy Astor, New York,
no. 51 (first version)

Geoffrey Clements, New York,
nos. 10, 11, 12, 14, 15, 16,
24, 35, 37, 44, 50

Sherwin Greenberg,
McGranahan and May Inc., Buffalo,
nos. 8, 33, 39, 49

Robert McElroy, New York,
nos. 25, 30

Peter Moore, New York,
photo of Claes Oldenburg

Eric Pollitzer, New York,
nos. 7, 9

Nathan Rabin, New York,
nos. 1, 2, 3, 4, 5, 13, 17, 26, 27,
28, 36, 48, 51 (second version), 52, 54

Eric Sutherland, Minneapolis,
no. 32

Ron Vickers, Toronto,
nos. 31, 34, 38, 53, 57

PRODUCTION

Design: Frank Newfeld

Production: Frank Newfeld Studio

Typesetting: LinoComp

Printing: Mirror Offset Co.

PRINTED AND BOUND IN CANADA